The rules book

By the same author

Start to Win (*Adlard Coles Limited*)
Dinghy Team Racing (*Adlard Coles Limited*)

Dedication : To my mother and father who
taught me the first rules I knew.

Eric
Twiname

The rules
book

The 1977–80 Yacht Racing Rules explained

ADLARD COLES LIMITED
GRANADA PUBLISHING
London Toronto Sydney New York

Published by Granada Publishing in
Adlard Coles Limited 1977

Granada Publishing Limited
Frogmore, St Albans, Hertfordshire AL2 2NF
and
3 Upper James Street, London W1R 4BP
1221 Avenue of the Americas, New York, NY 10020 USA
117 York Street, Sydney, NSW 2000, Australia
100 Skyway Avenue, Toronto, Ontario, Canada M9W 3A6
Trio City, Coventry Street, Johannesburg, 2001, South Africa

ISBN 0 229 11579 9

Printed in Great Britain by
Fletcher & Son Ltd, Norwich

CONTENTS

ACKNOWLEDGEMENTS

Very many people have helped me with this book, which is the culmination of seven years' occasional writing, lecturing and thinking about the rules and twenty years using them. I can't remember everyone who has helped, let alone thank them all. But a few people have been especially helpful.

Some of the interpretations and the idea of using an almost comic-strip presentation first appeared in my articles for *Yachts and Yachting* whose readers very usefully pounced on my interpretative mistakes. The International Yacht Racing Union kindly allowed us to reprint sections of the racing rules, and the Royal Yachting Association gave me a unique opportunity to sharpen up my wits and rule knowledge by asking me to join their racing rules committee three years ago.

The manuscript came in for a hard time under the perceptive eyes of Bryan Willis, Andrew Pool, Graham Donald, Nick Martin and the National Sailing coach, Bob Bond, who checked the book for its use in teaching and for ease of understanding. The chairman of the IYRU and RYA racing rules committees, Gerald Sambrooke Sturgess, was kind enough to read and correct the manuscript as carefully as if he had written it himself. Almost all their suggestions and corrections have been worked into the book.

Clive Gordon and the Parkway Design Group produced the quite superb design and layout with more than just professional competence and imagination. They were also amazingly patient.

Everyone I have dealt with in Adlard Coles and Granada, especially Jeremy Howard-Williams, Bruce Thomas and Rab MacWilliam, have responded with exceptional warmth and enthusiasm to the project. But my biggest debt is to Oliver Freeman. It was Oliver, when managing editor, who persuaded me to write the book and shaped it with me at every step of the way, even when he no longer worked for the company. Did I say my biggest debt? I was forgetting Jill.

To all of you who have helped, thank you.

Eric Twiname
March 1977

LEARNING THE
RULES

Learning the Rules

The rules of sailing are complex. There's no getting away from that. But there are ways of making rule knowledge much more accessible and the rules themselves easier to understand. This book is written very much with those two aims in mind.

Anyone who races sailing boats needs to know something about the rules. To begin with you only need know enough to get a boat round the course without fouling the others. Later the rules become tactically important because they define what moves you are allowed to make when trying to overtake other boats and, just as important, what tricks other people might legitimately use in trying to overtake you.

So the crucial point about learning the sailing rules is that your knowledge needs to be a working knowledge. There is little point in learning the rules merely to be able to quote chapter and verse. That won't help you on the water, whereas a good working knowledge certainly will, since rule knowledge is a vital department of your racing skills – as important as knowledge of wind and weather.

The International Yacht Racing Union's (IYRU) racing rule book is something most people approach at best reluctantly. For one thing it's usually only approached at all when you've got a problem. Which puts it immediately into the category of garages, police stations and dentists. But with the difference that most times you turn to the rule book you will find something that either you can't quite understand or that contradicts something you thought you did know.

This book therefore approaches the whole problem the other way round, starting from the real live situations that you're liable to come across while racing. So rather than looking for a rule which might apply to the situation in question, you can turn straight to that situation and read which rule applies, how it applies and why it applies. To make this possible, the situations are arranged here, not to the basic logic of the IYRU rule book, but to a logic based on your perception of situations as you meet them on the water.

There are several things that anyone who knows anything at all about sailing will be able to tell you about a collision or near miss, whether they have ever seen a rule book or not. The first thing they'll be able to say is whereabouts on the course the incident happened. They shouldn't find it too difficult either, to say which tacks the boats were on or whether they were tacking or gybing. And already, by answering these questions correctly, over 90 per cent of racing incidents can be eliminated and we are left with, at most, 10 per cent. The sections of the book have therefore been arranged to correspond to parts of the course, with subdivisions into incidents where boats are on opposite tacks, on the same tack, tacking or gybing.

In this way, when you are trying to unravel the rights and wrongs of a particular incident, you can quickly home in on the relevant 5 or 10 per cent of possible incidents. Among these, the one you want will be easy to find. Having found it, you can read why one boat is in the right and the other in the wrong, why a particular rule applies, which rule that is and, on difficult points, which appeals cases support the interpretation. The rule referred to can then be looked up in the IYRU rule book (parts I, IV, V and VI are reproduced in the back of this book, starting on page 93).

So far I have only mentioned the book's use in providing a post-mortem analysis after a rule infringement. But if you're a racing helmsman you constantly need to know just what you can do during a race without infringing any rules. You can certainly build up this knowledge by tearing around the course hitting other boats and being protested against afterwards, but by far the best way to learn is to keep your rule knowledge running in advance of your sailing skills.

Some right-of-way problems are much more common than others, so the situations dealt with here are graded so that you can, if you like, sit down and work up your rule knowledge to a level that fits in with your other racing abilities.

The incidents and situations interpreted in the book are graded on three levels. These levels are set at roughly what you should know for:

    1. rules everyone who races should know (dealt with on pages 5 to 9)

    2. racing at the top end of a club fleet

    3. top-level national and international competition and team racing

For the purpose of learning the rules, the book should not be read from cover to cover in the usual way. That would be too big a bite at once and probably pretty confusing, unless you already knew the rules quite well. Instead, the best approach is to decide what level of rule knowledge you want from the book beforehand, then to ignore everything listed as being beyond the level you've set yourself.

Take the example of a helmsman who has raced for a couple of seasons, and who wants to improve his rule knowledge so that he is at least on a par with the people who are winning his club races. His approach to learning would be to read all items marked by one boat (but not those marked by two boats), checking back to any rules referred to, but ignoring the appeal case references.

If you work in this way you needn't read from the front of the book to the back, but will learn faster by picking a particular section – mark-rounding from an offwind leg, for example, – and first studying only that section, rather than trying to take in too much at once. Re-reading, dipping into the book at random – but not yet reading beyond the level you've set yourself – are all useful parts of the learning process. For really keen groups of people, and particularly for children, quizzes are an obvious way of livening up the process.

Learning is also speeded up considerably by using the book as a reference after racing to check the rights and wrongs of any incidents or near misses you experienced during the race. When using the book in this way, of course, you would not restrict yourself to the grading levels, since an incident you want to know about might be one of those rare ones in group 3.

One important word of warning, though. What may look like two identical situations in different sections of the book will sometimes have opposite interpretations. This is because the position on the course is crucial. For example, when two boats collide within two lengths of a mark, the boat in the wrong is liable to be the one that is in the right if you take the mark away and have them in open water on a leg of the course. It is vital to make sure you read and bear in mind the leg of course the boats are on–which is why that information is printed at the top of every page.

The interpretations are, as far as possible, not my own but those of the IYRU, the RYA (Royal Yachting Association) and the NAYRU (North American Yacht Racing Union – now the USYRU). Throughout I have included references to their most useful published appeals, so anyone can look these up if they want to. At protest meetings – whether you are on the committee or one of the warring parties – the relevant appeal case placed on the table is usually decisive – and gratifying. You are instantly a rule expert. No longer is it a question of 'my opinion is this...' but 'this is what the definitive IYRU, RYA or NAYRU appeal says'. Which is difficult for a protest committee to refute, or for a competitor who has just been disqualified to argue about.

The IYRU appeal cases are accepted as definitive anywhere (except in the very rare case of a more recent published national appeal conflicting, when the national appeal would apply in that country). The RYA appeals apply in British clubs and classes and any others under the RYA's jurisdiction; the NAYRU appeals apply only in the USA and Canada. Elsewhere national appeals of the country concerned govern, but in the absence of a national or IYRU appeal on a point of interpretation for races held outside Britain or the USA, an RYA or NAYRU appeal which clarified the point would usually be accepted by a protest committee in that country. The national authority would always have the chance of reversing the decision on appeal – if the dispute went that far.

The rules themselves are revised once every four years and those used in this edition are valid until 1981. These rules together with the RYA prescriptions can be bought in a booklet from the Royal Yachting Association, Victoria Way, Woking, Surrey GU21 1EQ. So can the RYA appeals cases. The IYRU racing rules alone and its appeals can be bought from the IYRU at 60 Knightsbridge, London SW1X 7JX, and NAYRU appeals from the USYRU, 31st Floor, 1133 Avenue of the Americas, 43/44th Streets, New York, NY, 10036.

THE RULES
EVERYONE WHO
RACES
SHOULD KNOW

An understanding of these first
few pages of introduction to the
rules enables a racing helmsman
to keep out of trouble and
provides the logical framework
which underlies all the right of
way rules, however complex.
These are the most important
four pages in the book.

The sailing rules are meant to prevent collisions. So when boats collide, or when a right-of-way boat is forced to steer clear, the boat in the wrong should be penalised. The voluntary penalty is retirement from the race or, when 720 degree penalties are in force, two full penalty turns. If a helmsman in the wrong does not take the voluntary penalty soon after the incident, another competitor or the race organisers may lodge a protest. In the protest meeting the boat in the wrong is disqualified.

The basic right-of-way code is quite simple, but it is important to know that the right-of-way in open water is fundamentally different from that at marks of the course or other obstructions.

Basic right-of-way in open water

When neither boat is about to sail round a mark but are both in open water:

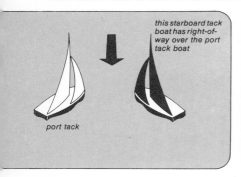

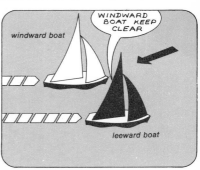

1. A boat on port tack keeps clear of a boat on starboard tack (rule 36).

2. A windward boat keeps clear of a leeward boat (rule 37.1).

3. A boat which is tacking or gybing keeps clear of one that isn't (rule 41).

4. A boat clear astern of another keeps clear of the one ahead when they are both on the same tack (rule 37.2).

Basic right-of-way at a windward mark

At a windward mark – that is a mark of the course which you have been tacking to reach – the basics are:

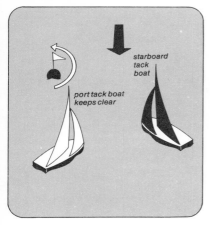

1. When on opposite tacks, take the mark away and apply the principles as in open water (rule 42.1(c) and 36).

2. When on the same tack, the boat next to the mark must be given room to round by the boat outside (rule 42.1 (a)).

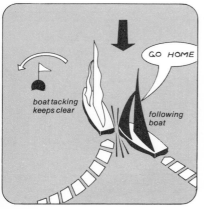

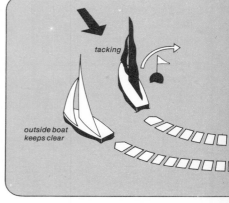

3. When a boat is tacking round the mark, she must keep clear of any following boat (rule 42.2(b)) but any boat outside her must give her room (rule 42.1(a)).

7

Basic right-of-way at an offwind mark

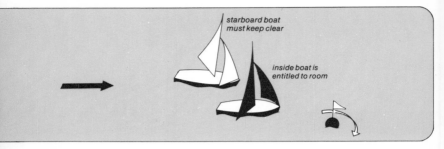

At an offwind mark – that is one you have sailed to on a close reach, broad reach or run – the basics are:

1. The boat on the inside at the mark must be given room to round (rule 42.1(a)). The port and starboard and windward and leeward rules (36 and 37) do not apply here.

2. A boat which approaches the mark clear ahead of another has the right to gybe round the mark; the other boat must keep clear (rule 42. 2(a)).

3. The boat on the inside must make a tidy job of the rounding and not round so wide that she sails into a boat that is giving her room.

Basic rights before and at the start

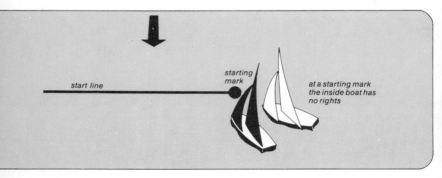

The rules before the start are slightly different in some details from those after the start. Collisions are common before the start, and it is important to realise that if you are either out of control or are preoccupied in adjusting a halyard, you can be penalised in a collision with a boat which has right-of-way. So if you're going to mess about with your boat just before the start, make sure you're on starboard tack. The racing rules usually apply from 5 minutes before the starting signal.

At a starting mark an inside boat has no right to room (rule 42.4).

The luffing rule

windward boat
must keep clear

the leeward boat
has the right to luff

There is another rule which is worth knowing about right from the beginning: this is the luffing rule (rule 38). When you're overtaking another boat to windward the leeward helmsman has the right to protect his wind by throwing his boat head to wind as sharply as he likes. If he hits you, you are the one who'll be penalised for the collision. A luff may only be done slowly before the start (rule 40).

DEFINITIONS

The rules are built on simple and
precise ideas; these are the
building blocks and they must
be understood if the full meaning
of the rules is to become clear.

Racing

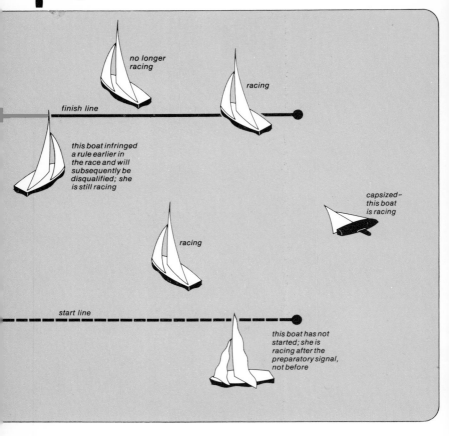

no longer
racing

racing

finish line

this boat infringed
a rule earlier in
the race and will
subsequently be
disqualified; she
is still racing

capsized –
this boat
is racing

racing

start line

this boat has not
started; she is
racing after the
preparatory signal,
not before

The international racing rules apply to boats which are racing or about to race. Penalties for infringing the rules come into force after the preparatory signal (usually 5 minutes before the starting signal) and apply to a boat until she has finished and cleared the finish line. A boat may then only be penalised under the rules for seriously hindering a boat which is still racing.

A boat which infringes a rule, continues racing and is later disqualified after a protest does not lose her right-of-way status during the race. She is racing throughout and carries exactly the same rights under the rules as other boats racing (IYRU appeal case 2).

Port tack and starboard tack

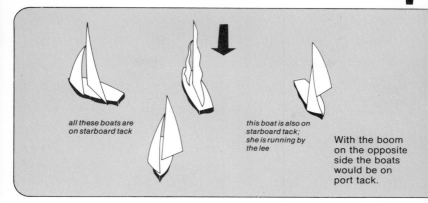

all these boats are
on starboard tack

this boat is also on
starboard tack;
she is running by
the lee

With the boom
on the opposite
side the boats
would be on
port tack.

A boat is on starboard tack when her mainsail is on her port side. Conversely, a boat is on port tack when her mainsail is on her starboard side. Helmsmen who have problems knowing which tack they are on can usefully paint 'starboard tack' on the starboard side of the boom and 'port tack' on the port side. It saves having to think.

Close-hauled and free

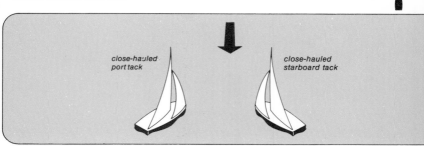

close-hauled
port tack

close-hauled
starboard tack

The term 'close-hauled' defines a direction of sailing in relation to the wind; this is different for different classes of boat and to a lesser degree among boats of the same class. The official rule book definition reads: 'A yacht is close-hauled when sailing by the wind as close as she can lie with advantage in working to windward'.

The terms 'beating', 'beating to windward' and 'on the wind' are all sometimes used to mean close-hauled.

Windward and leeward

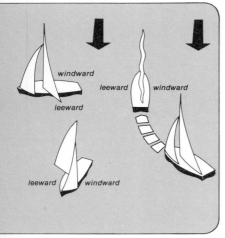

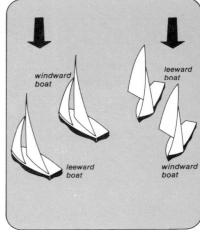

The leeward side of a boat is the side that the mainsail is being carried; or if head to wind, on the side the mainsail was before she luffed head to wind. The opposite side is the windward side.

When two boats are overlapped on the same tack the leeward one is the one on the other's leeward side. The other boat is the windward one.

Luffing

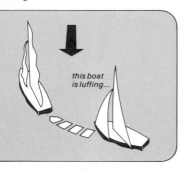

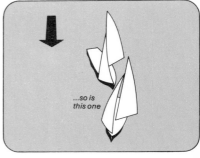

A boat which is luffing is altering course towards the wind. Other phrases commonly used (though not in the rules) to mean the same as luffing are: 'hardening up', 'pointing up' and 'putting the helm down'.

Bearing away

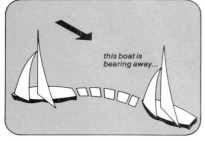

this boat is bearing away...

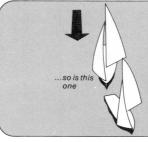

...so is this one

A boat which is bearing away is altering course away from the wind. Bearing away stops when the boat begins to gybe. Other phrases commonly used (though not in the rules) to mean the same as bearing away are: 'bearing off', 'bearing down', 'freeing off' and 'putting the helm up'.

Tacking

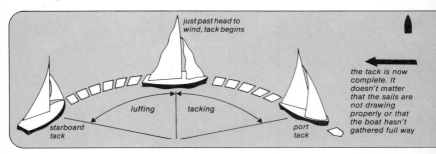

just past head to wind, tack begins

the tack is now complete. It doesn't matter that the sails are not drawing properly or that the boat hasn't gathered full way

luffing   tacking

starboard tack

port tack

When people talk about tacking they usually mean the whole manoeuvre from first putting the helm down to getting under way on the new tack. The rule book definition is much narrower than this. The boat first luffs, and her tack is not defined as beginning until after she has passed through the eye of the wind. When beating to windward, tacking continues until the boat is close-hauled on the new tack.

When a boat is not beating, tacking continues until she is on a course on which the mainsail fills.

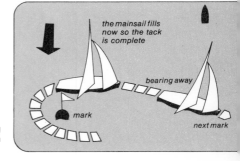

the mainsail fills now so the tack is complete

bearing away

mark

next mark

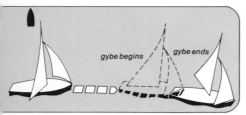

gybe begins · gybe ends

Gybing

Gybing happens much more quickly than tacking. The gybe begins when, with the wind aft, the boom crosses the centreline; it ends when the mainsail has filled on the other tack.

Overlapped, clear astern and clear ahead

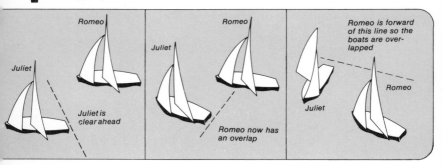

Romeo · Juliet · Juliet is clear ahead

Romeo · Juliet · Romeo now has an overlap

Romeo is forward of this line so the boats are overlapped · Romeo · Juliet

'A yacht is clear astern of another when her hull and equipment in normal position are abaft an imaginary line projected abeam from the aftermost point of the other's hull and equipment in normal position. The other yacht is clear ahead...' (Definition in Part I of the rule book.)

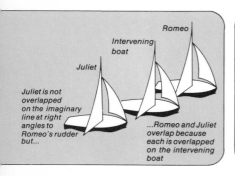

Romeo · Intervening boat · Juliet · Juliet is not overlapped on the imaginary line at right angles to Romeo's rudder but... · ...Romeo and Juliet overlap because each is overlapped on the intervening boat

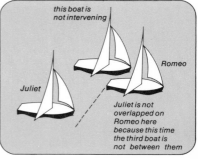

this boat is not intervening · Romeo · Juliet · Juliet is not overlapped on Romeo here because this time the third boat is not between them

'The yachts overlap if neither is clear astern; or if, although one is clear astern, an intervening yacht overlaps both of them...' (Definition.)

Obstruction

'An obstruction is any object, including a vessel under way, large enough to require a
yacht, if not less than one overall length away from it, to make a substantial alteration of
course to pass on one side or the other, or any object which can be passed on one side
only, including a buoy when the yacht in question cannot safely pass between it and the
shoal or object which it marks'. (Definition.)

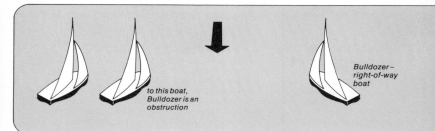

to this boat,
Bulldozer is an
obstruction

Bulldozer –
right-of-way
boat

Obstructions include shorelines, heavy patches of weed, fishing nets, shallows,
moored boats, motor boats, crusing boats and, in some situations, other boats racing.
Right-of-way boats and boats which refuse to give way, are out of control or capsized
all rate as obstructions.

Mark

'A mark is any object specified in the sailing instructions which a yacht must round or
pass on a required side. Every ordinary part of a mark ranks as part of it, including a
flag, flagpole, boom or hoisted boat, but excluding ground tackle and any object either
accidentally or temporarily attached to the mark'. (Definition.)

A dinghy tied to a mark does not count as part of the mark, unless specified in the
sailing instructions (RYA appeal case 7 1971); nor does anything that has accidentally
become attached to it or is only temporarily attached.

A mark's ground tackle is not counted as part of the mark (NAYRU appeal case 3),
but when a boat runs into the mooring line and is drawn onto any part of the mark,
above or below water, she is counted as having hit the mark (NAYRU appeal case 59).

Windward leg

A windward leg or, as it's often
called, a beat, is a leg of the
course which is sailed close-
hauled, and on which the mark
that ends the leg can not be
reached without putting in at
least one tack.

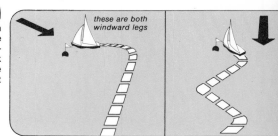

these are both
windward legs

▲ Offwind leg
Any leg which is not a windward leg is an offwind leg. A free leg (the rule book's term) or a downwind leg mean exactly the same.

▲ Starting and finishing
Starting is dealt with at the beginning of the special section on starting (page 21) and finishing is dealt with at the beginning of the special section on finishing (page 78).

▲ Postponement, abandonment and cancellation
A postponed race is one which is not started at its scheduled time and which can be sailed at any time the race committee may decide.

Abandonment and cancellation are often confused with one another because their special meanings as defined in the sailing rules are not those of everyday use. An abandoned race is one which the race committee calls off at any time after the start and which may be re-sailed at its discretion. A race which is cancelled before its scheduled start cannot be sailed. A race which is cancelled after it has been started cannot be re-sailed.

▲ Collision
A boat which fails to keep clear of another collides. A collision happens when there is contact between any part of one boat (including all rigging, sails and sheets) or her crew and part of another boat or her crew (IYRU case 72).

▲ Proper course

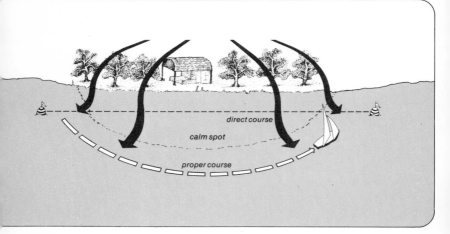

direct course

calm spot

proper course

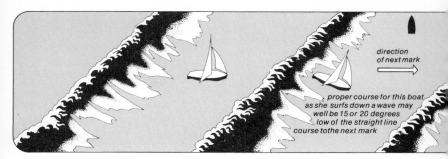

direction
of next mark

proper course for this boat
as she surfs down a wave may
well be 15 or 20 degrees
low of the straight line
course to the next mark

'A proper course is any course which a yacht might sail after the starting signal, in the absence of other yacht or yachts affected, to finish as quickly as possible...'. (Definition.) The reference to other yacht or yachts affected means that a helmsman is not sailing his proper course if, for example, he bears away solely to gain a tactical advantage over a boat or boats just behind or overlapping him.

Proper course refers to the course the boat makes good and not the direction she is pointing (RYA case 9 1969 and NAYRU case 79).

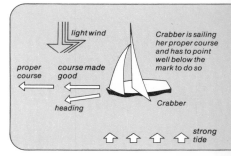

light wind

Crabber is sailing
her proper course
and has to point
well below the
mark to do so

proper
course

course made
good

heading

Crabber

There is no proper course before the starting signal.

strong
tide

Helmsman

Someone of either sex who is steering a sailing boat. Referred to as he.

Yacht

The IYRU rule book uses the word 'yacht' to mean any sailing boat. In the official language of the rule book Optimists, Lasers and 505s, for example, are all yachts, though no-one who sails them would normally refer to them as yachts – except in jest.

THE START

The starting period covered in this section runs from the moment a boat receives her preparatory signal to the moment after the starting signal when she starts.

◢ Timing of starts

A race is started by a 10 minute warning signal, a 5 minute preparatory signal and the start signal. If there is an error of timing between the 10 minute and 5 minute signals, the starting signal must follow exactly 5 minutes after the preparatory signal – unless the race is then postponed (rule 4.4(d)). A national authority or a race committee through its sailing instructions may specify different timings. This often happens in team races where a 6 minute, 3 minute, start sequence is often used (rule 4.4(a) and (b)).

The timing is taken from the visual signals, not from the sound signals (rule 4.8).

The racing rules come into force with the back-up of penalties at the 5 minute preparatory signal (definition of racing).

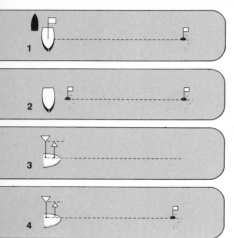

Start lines

A start line must be one of the following:

(a) A line between a mark and a mast on the committee boat or place clearly identified in the sailing instructions (1).

(b) A line between two marks (2).

(c) The extension of a line through two stationary posts (3), which may have a mark at or near its outer limit, that boats must pass inside (4).

◢◢ On starting lines of types (1), (3) and (4) an inner distance mark, clearly defined in the sailing instructions, may be laid. Boats must then pass between this mark and the outer distance mark. These floating marks should never be laid on the pre-start side of the line (that is, behind the line) but always exactly on or just over it, otherwise they do not rate as starting marks.

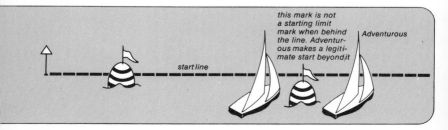

this mark is not a starting limit mark when behind the line. Adventurous makes a legitimate start beyond it

Adventurous

start line

Over the line at the start

When any part of a boat, her sails, rigging, equipment or crew is on the course side of the start line at the starting signal the boat is a premature starter (rule 8).

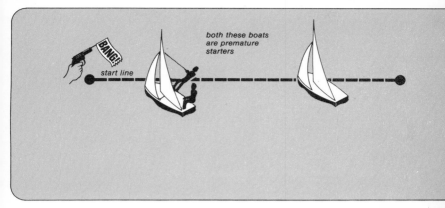

both these boats are premature starters

start line

If the race is being started for the first time (that is, the whole fleet has not just been recalled) the race officer must make a sound signal and leave the class warning signal at the dip, but on view. If recall numbers have been issued, the offending boats' recall numbers must be displayed instead of leaving the class flag at the dip (rule 8.2).

A boat which has started prematurely must now re-start or be disqualified – or take whatever alternative penalty the sailing instructions may specify. But if this recall procedure, or any other specified procedure in the class rules or sailing instructions which overrides this one, is not followed, a premature starter cannot be penalised for her error (IYRU case 30). A premature starter, for example, is not required to go back and re-start when the visual signal is not accompanied by the prescribed sound signal (rule 8.2 and IYRU case 70).

When a recalled boat has returned completely to the pre-start side of the start line, her recall number will be lowered and she can start correctly. If the race officer slips up and removes the recall number too soon, the boat is entitled to start the race – even though she may not have re-crossed the start line. When there are no recall numbers the dipped flag is lowered once the last of the premature starters has returned to the pre-start side of the line, or before that if the race committee reckons the flag has been dipped for a reasonable time (rule 8.2(b)).

It is vital to check through sailing instructions carefully for the starting procedure because race committees are allowed to write their own (rule 8.2(c)).

Any boat anchored before the start with part of her ground tackle over the start line at the start signal becomes a premature starter because the anchor and warp is part of the boat's equipment (rule 8.2).

If the race is being started after a general recall, any boat whose hull, equipment or crew is on the course side of the start line during the minute before the start must sail round one end of the line to start. She may not just dip back over the line as on a first start (rule 51.1(c)).

Hitting a starting mark

A boat which collides with a starting mark after the preparatory signal and before starting can stay in the race provided she re-rounds the mark after starting (rule 52). If the collision happens after starting, the re-rounding may be done immediately, provided there is room (but a boat doing a penalty re-rounding has no rights over other boats starting correctly).

The sailing instructions may exclude use of penalty mark re-rounding (rule 52.2). The offender would then be required to retire.

720 degree penalty for an infringement before the start signal

When the sailing instructions specify that the 720 degree penalty is in force the turns may be done for an infringement that happens before the start signal. But the turns must be made after the start signal and at the first reasonable opportunity. So many places are lost by doing 720 degree turns at the start that the penalty is therefore much more severe for pre-starting signal incidents than for incidents that happen later in the race. (720 degree turns are dealt with in detail on page 86.)

Anchored, moored, tied up or still ashore

A boat may be disqualified for being ashore, moored or tied up after the preparatory (5 minute) signal (rule 63). If she doesn't sail about in the vicinity of the start line between the preparatory and starting signals, she is counted as a non-starter (rule 50 and IYRU case 34).

If she does get to the vicinity of the line before the starting signal, she must be ranked as a starter (rule 50) and can only be disqualified under rule 63 after a proper protest hearing or with the agreement of the offender. A helmsman cannot exonerate himself under this rule by taking any alternative penalties since they only apply to the right-of-way rules in Part IV of the rule book. Rule 63 is in Part V.

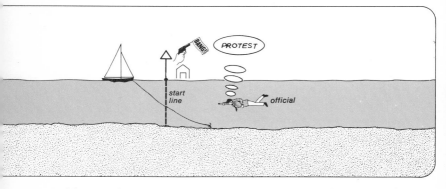

A boat may be anchored after the preparatory signal or held by a member of the crew standing in the water, and no rule is broken (rule 63). However, if an anchor is over the line at the start, the boat is reckoned to be a premature starter.

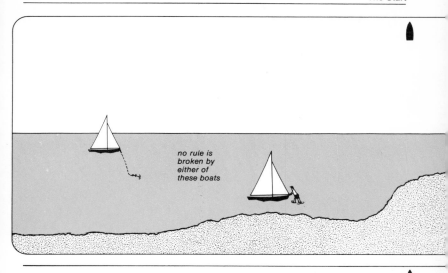

no rule is
broken by
either of
these boats

General recall

When the race officer can't pick out all the premature starters, or when the start is unsatisfactory in some other way, he can abandon the start by flying the First Substitute and making two more sound signals after the starting signal.

First
Substitute

The procedure for the re-start is then:
1. First Substitute is lowered to the accompaniment of a sound signal.
2. A new warning signal is made.

Once again, though, the sailing instructions may give a different procedure. This would have precedence over the IYRU recommended procedure.

Any boat which commits a foul on the abandoned start is not penalised for it on any subsequent starts unless the sailing instructions specifically say so (and that is very rare except in unmanageably large starts).

Postponment

A race may be postponed by flying the Answering Pendant. The race will then be started after the scheduled time at the discretion of the race committee. The warning signal is made one minute after the Answering Pendant is lowered.

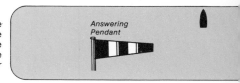

Answering
Pendant

RIGHT OF WAY

▲ Starting
A boat starts when any part of her hull, crew or equipment first crosses the start line after the start signal in the direction of the first mark, provided she has no penalty obligations to fulfill. (Definition of starting in Part I of the rules.)

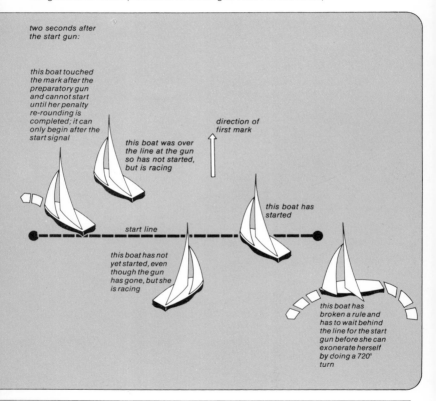

two seconds after the start gun:

this boat touched the mark after the preparatory gun and cannot start until her penalty re-rounding is completed; it can only begin after the start signal

this boat was over the line at the gun so has not started, but is racing

direction of first mark

this boat has started

start line

this boat has not yet started, even though the gun has gone, but she is racing

this boat has broken a rule and has to wait behind the line for the start gun before she can exonerate herself by doing a 720° turn

▲ No room at a starting mark
When approaching the line to start (but not at any other time) a windward boat (white) is not entitled to demand room from any leeward boat (black) at a starting mark (rule 42.4).

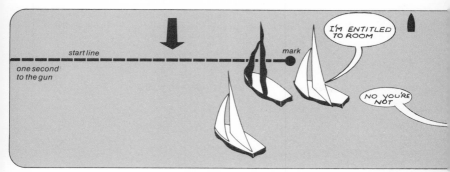

But after the starting signal the leeward boat is not entitled to squeeze the windward boat out at the mark by sailing either:

1. above (that is, upwind of) the course to the first mark *or*
2. above close-hauled (rule 42.4).

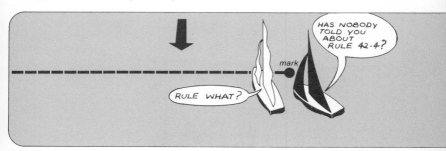

The mark must be a starting mark and surrounded by navigable water for this ruling to apply.

In the to-ing and fro-ing before the start, though, a windward boat is entitled to room at a starting mark. The 'no water' rule applies only 'when approaching the line to start'.

At the other end of the start line the leeward boat is entitled to room. (Rule 42.4 refers only to passing 'to leeward of a starting mark'.) The black boat here is about to pass to windward of the mark and is therefore entitled to room (rule 42.4 and 35(b)).

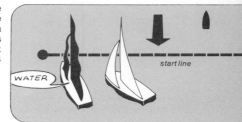

The position is quite different if the starting mark cannot be sailed round or the line's length is limited by, say, a pier. A windward boat is then entitled to room at that mark or pier (rule 42.4 does not apply; rule 42.1(a) does).

Altering course to start

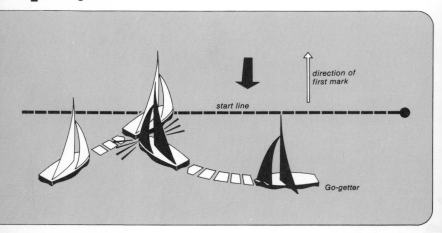

A boat which is altering course to start does not have to worry about any non-right-of-way boats which are on the opposite tack, whereas at any other time in the race (except at marks) she would (rule 35(b)).

Go-getter is altering course to start and white is in the wrong. If she were not starting, **Go-getter,** as right-of-way boat, would be in the wrong for altering course in a way that obstructs a boat which was keeping clear.

Luffing before the start

The luffing rules that apply before a boat starts are fundamentally different from those that apply later. A luff may not be fast before she starts and the acquisition of luffing rights is quite different.

After the preparatory signal (5 minute) but before she has started and cleared the start line:

1. She may luff a windward boat slowly and in such a way that the windward boat has 'room and opportunity to keep clear' (rule 40).

2. The leeward boat has the right to luff as high as head to wind (again slowly) when the windward boat is at or aft of the 'mast abeam' position – regardless of how the two boats came together (rule 40).

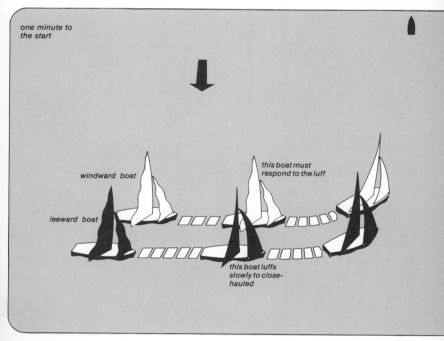

one minute to
the start

windward boat

leeward boat

this boat must
respond to the luff

this boat luffs
slowly to close-
hauled

The windward boat has not dropped behind the 'mast abeam' position (explained on page 72), so the leeward boat may not luff about close-hauled.

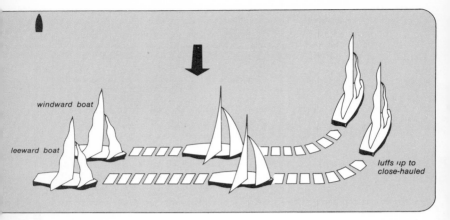

The leeward boat here is entitled to carry on luffing slowly until she is head to wind – provided the windward boat doesn't move forward of the 'mast abeam' position and provided the windward boat has 'room and opportunity to keep clear' (rules 40 and 38.4).

If, for example, the windward boat were idling when the luff began, she would require time to gather way and respond to the luff. The leeward boat has to give her this opportunity. It is important to remember that the first movement of the windward boat's stern in responding to a luff is inevitably *towards* the leeward boat. The windward boat would not be disqualified in a pre-start luffing incident if she made every reasonable effort to avoid the leeward boat's slow luff from the moment the luff began.

3. A luff which is higher than close-hauled can be stopped by the windward helmsman if he reaches the 'mast abeam' position. He simply hails 'mast abeam' and the leeward boat must bear off onto a close-hauled course (rules 40 and 38.4).
4. When more than one boat is overlapped upwind the leeward boat may not luff higher than close-hauled unless she has the right to luff *all* the overlapped boats head to wind (rules 40 and 38.6).

5. A windward helmsman can hail to stop the leeward boat luffing when he can't respond because of an obstruction (rules 40 and 38.5). A starting mark surrounded by navigable water does not rate as a legitimate obstruction when starting to leeward of it. If you call for room at a starting mark to curtail a luff in that situation and are given it, you are penalised (rule 42.4).

◗ Over the line at the start

While a premature starter is sailing the course, she carries full rights. But at the moment she begins her manoeuvre to return, she loses the protection of the main right-of-way rules (rule 44).

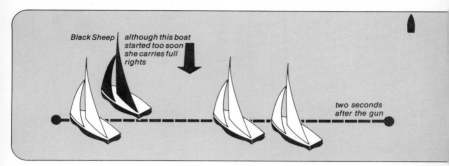

Now **Black Sheep** lets her sails flap to slow down. Her manoeuvre to return has begun and she must keep clear of all other boats.

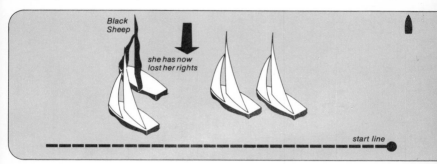

Once back on the pre-start side of the line **Black Sheep** gets back her rights, but she cannot make use of them immediately. She must allow boats over which she has right-of-way 'ample room and opportunity to keep clear' (rule 44.1(b)).

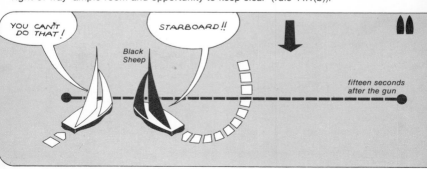

Black Sheep has acted too fast in claiming starboard rights. She has not given the port tack boat enough opportunity to keep clear. On this showing, **Black Sheep's** return to the fold would only be temporary.

After a general recall any boat whose hull, equipment or crew is on the course side of the start line or its extensions during the minute before the start must sail round one end of the line to start. She may not just dip back over the start line as on a first start (rule 51.1(c)). The sailing instructions, though, may override this rule.

Starting from the wrong side of the line

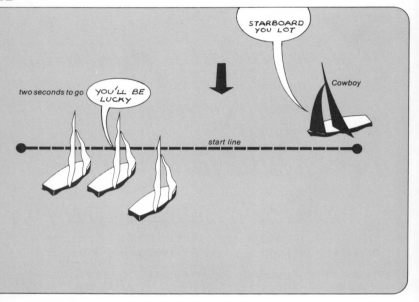

Cowboy enjoys right-of-way for 2 seconds more, than loses it as soon as the gun goes if she is caught with any part of the boat or crew on the wrong side of the line at the gun (rule 51.1(b) and 44.1(a)). If she gets behind the line in 2 seconds she has the right to head up and start as explained in 'Altering course to start', page 28.

But look out for any special starting provisions in the sailing instructions; they may override the IYRU rules that apply here.

Overtaking to leeward
This is very common before and at the start, though the rules that apply are exactly the same as would apply at any other time in the race.

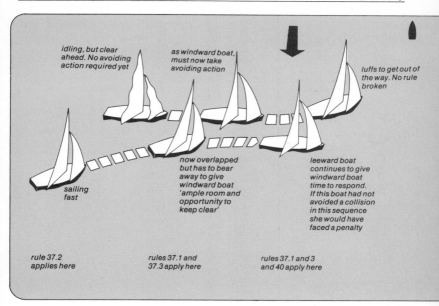

idling, but clear ahead. No avoiding action required yet

as windward boat, must now take avoiding action

luffs to get out of the way. No rule broken

sailing fast

now overlapped but has to bear away to give windward boat 'ample room and opportunity to keep clear'

leeward boat continues to give windward boat time to respond. If this boat had not avoided a collision in this sequence she would have faced a penalty

rule 37.2 applies here

rules 37.1 and 37.3 apply here

rules 37.1 and 3 and 40 apply here

'Ample room and opportunity' (rule 37.3) means more than just 'sufficient', and the benefit of any doubt must go to the windward boat.

Overtaking a wayless boat

The wayless boat is an obstruction to **Rapide**. **Wayless** need not begin to take avoiding action until **Rapide** overlaps. Therefore the initial avoiding action must be by **Rapide**. Any boat overlapped to leeward of **Rapide (Oblivious)** must keep clear if she's to avoid penalty – even when **Rapide** fails to call 'water' and **Oblivious'** crew doesn't see the wayless boat (rules 37.3 and 42.1(a) and NAYRU case 46).

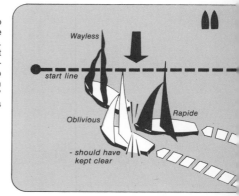

Wayless

start line

Oblivious

Rapide

- should have kept clear

WINDWARD LEG

A windward leg is one that a
boat can only complete by
putting in at least one tack.

OPPOSITE TACKS

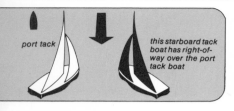

port tack

this starboard tack boat has right-of-way over the port tack boat

Port and starboard

A port tack boat gives way to a starboard tack boat (rule 36).

When there is no collision and a close-hauled starboard tack boat bears away to miss the port boat's stern, the onus of proof is on the port tack helmsman to show that the starboard boat would have missed had she held her course (RYA case 1 1973 and NAYRU case 32).

The port tack helmsman may hail 'hold your course' but this hail is not binding on the starboard boat, which can still bear away to miss and protest (NAYRU case 137). In dinghies, though, it is no bad thing for the starboard helmsman to hold his course in these circumstances. A rudder or transom clipped saves any argument.

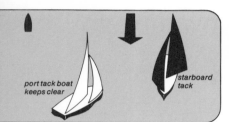

port tack boat keeps clear

starboard tack

A starboard tack boat sailing free has right-of-way over a close-hauled port tack boat, so long as the starboard tacker does not alter course in a way that prevents the port tack boat keeping clear (rules 35 and 36).

HAVE YOU NEVER HEARD OF RULE 35?

STARBOARD!

Port and starboard when the starboard tack boat alters course

A port and starboard incident where the starboard tack boat alters course and hits – or claims she could have hit – a port tacker is quite different from the straight-forward port and starboard case above. This situation is controlled by rule 35, which is designed to deny *carte blanche* to alter course and hit give way boats.

The white boat on starboard is in the wrong because she altered course when the port boat was properly keeping clear. Nor can an offwind starboard tack boat legitimately alter course to hit a port tack boat that is sailing a course to keep clear.

Even when there is a windshift, rule 35 can override the basic port and starboard rule (IYRU case 52, RYA case 5 1974 and NAYRU case 157). To use the windshift as a defence at a protest hearing, black would have to establish to the committee's satisfaction that she was clearly going to cross white before the windshift complicated matters.

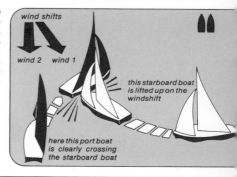

Port and starboard when starboard tack boat has just tacked

'A yacht shall neither tack nor gybe into a position which will give her right of way unless she does so far enough from a yacht on a tack to enable this yacht to keep clear without having to begin to alter her course until after the tack or gybe has been completed' (rule 41.2).

The boat which has just tacked (**Jack-in-the-box**) has the onus of satisfying the race committee that the tack was completed far enough from the other boat (rule 41.3). Protest committees are too often apt to place the onus on the port tack boat, merely because the port and starboard rule is basic. In cases like this one they would be wrong to do that.

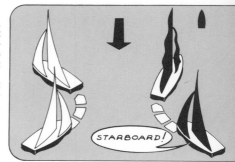

Calling 'starboard'

There is no obligation to call 'starboard', but anybody who makes a habit of not hailing would soon become pretty unpopular – particularly when tacking onto starboard a few lengths away from a port tack boat.

The starboard tack boat on the right breaks no rule by hailing 'starboard', putting the port tack boat about, then tacking.

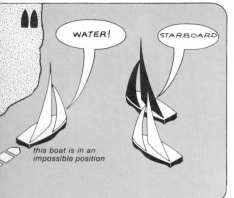

this boat is in an
impossible position

Opposite tack boat requiring room for an obstruction

There is, curiously, no way that a port tack boat which is prevented from tacking by an obstruction can legitimately force starboard tack boats to tack and give her room. Only when she calls for room before tacking can she put the starboard tackers about without infringing the rules (rule 43, explained opposite). Otherwise the port and starboard rule (36) applies, in spite of the fact that the port tack boat's only escape may be to capsize quickly or go aground.

SAME TACK

 Windward and leeward

When two boats are beating on the same tack and the one to windward is not sailing as close to the wind as the leeward one, the windward boat must keep clear (rule 37.1).

windward boat

The leeward boat may not sail above her proper course (close-hauled here) unless she has luffing rights (rule 38.1 and 2).

If the leeward boat has come up from clear astern, she must allow the windward boat 'ample room and opportunity to keep clear' from the moment the overlap is established (rule 37.3). This may mean that the leeward boat has to bear off initially, but the windward boat is required to respond by luffing above her close-hauled course if necessary. Again, the initial onus to keep clear is on the boat which has newly acquired right-of-way (the leeward one).

The crew or helmsman of the leeward boat may not deliberately reach out, sit out or trapeze with the prime intention of hitting the windward boat (RYA case 9 1965). This is penalised under the fair sailing rule .

Luffing

The rule is exactly the same as for an off-wind leg (page 72). I should mention one situation, though, which only crops up on the beat; it represents a particularly sharp, but legitimate, use of the luffing rule.

From the moment one boat completes a tack a new set of rights comes in (rule 38.3). And if the leeward boat has luffing rights, she can luff as soon after the tack as she likes, and as sharply as she likes, up to head to wind (rule 38.1). Though she is not entitled to cause serious damage (rule 32).

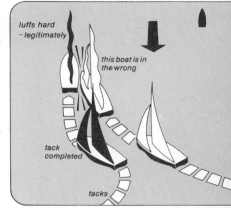

Bearing down

Provided the leeward boat isn't made to alter course to avoid hitting the windward boat, the windward boat may bear away below close-hauled as white does here.

This would not be allowed on an offwind leg because rule 39 (sailing below a proper course) forbids it, but that rule applies only to free legs, not beats. It is also worth remembering that it is the leg itself that counts, not the actual point of sailing, so if two boats have overstood a weather mark the windward one may bear down on the other since, although sailing free, they are still on the windward leg. (A windward leg is defined on page 17.)

Calling for room at a continuous obstruction

If **Mud Tickler** carries on she'll hit the shore; if she tacks she'll hit white. The rules provide a way out of this one provided both boats are on the same tack as they are here: **Mud Tickler** can hail 'water',

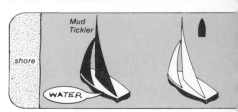

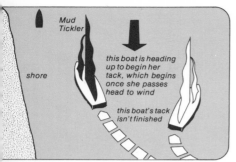

'shore room' or something similar at white before tacking. (But if she makes the call after tacking she'll be in trouble, as explained on page 38).

The white boat here must now respond either by immediately:

1. tacking *or*
2. hailing 'you tack' (rule 43.2).

If white chooses to tack immediately, **Mud Tickler** must begin to tack before white's tack is finished (rule 43.2(a)(i) and NAYRU case 108). But **Mud Tickler** is not entitled to hail and tack immediately into white (rule 43.2(a)(ii)).

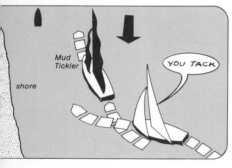

White may prefer to let **Mud Tickler** tack, keep out of her way and really squeeze into the shore herself. Then white must call 'you tack' and avoid **Mud Tickler.** The onus is now entirely on white to keep out of the way (rule 43.2(b)(ii) and (iii)).

Once white has made her 'you tack' call, **Mud Tickler** must tack immediately. If she doesn't she can be protested against – even if there is no collision (rule 43.2 (b)(i)).

The commonest problems in these situations come up when short tacking against a tide, and hinge on how far apart the boats need to be before the inshore boat's call for water is invalid. There is no set number of boat lengths – the distance will vary according to the conditions and the type of boat – but the criteria for deciding are quite clear. The inshore boat is not entitled to hail for water when:

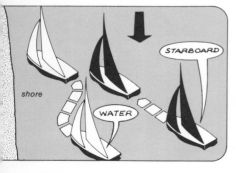

1. she can tack out from the shore and back again onto her original tack without tacking in the other boat's water *or*
2. she can clearly tack and bear off behind the other boat without colliding.

The white boat here is able to tack out from the shore and back onto her original tack without tacking in black's water. Black was therefore justified in not responding to the 'water' call. But the onus here is on black. It is very risky to refuse a call for water unless it is clearly a ludicrous one.

In this sequence, too, the call was dubious. Here the inshore boat did manage to get behind black, but if she hadn't been able to, black would have been in the wrong. Again, it was chancy to refuse the 'water' call. But white is required to tack and bear off astern of black, if that's possible (rule 43.1 and NAYRU case 108).

Calling for room at a non-continuous obstruction

A non-continuous obstruction is one which can be passed on either side and requires a boat not less than a length away to make a substantial alteration of course to miss it. Moored boats, miniscule islands, capsized boats, other boats sailing and motor boats may all be non-continuous obstructions (the definition is on page 17).

Once the 'water' call has been made here by black, white must respond exactly as in the section above (rule 43). The fact that white would have missed the obstruction anyway doesn't matter. Nor does it matter that black chose to tack rather than bear off and go to leeward of the obstruction. There is no rule which dictates that a boat should take the shortest route around an obstruction. Although if black would only need to make a small alteration of course when one length away, the rules don't allow her to call for water to tack; she must then make the course change, staying on the same tack (NAYRU case 81).

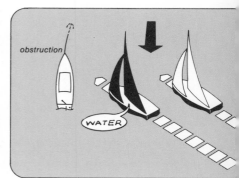

A starboard tack boat as an obstruction

One of the commonest obstructions to sea room is a starboard tack boat. Usually it will be close-hauled but it can be running free.

41

Stool-pigeon is entitled to hail for water to tack, and the white boat must either tack immediately or call 'you tack'. **Stool-pigeon** has to see this situation coming in good time or she'll be too late to call and won't be able to get out of the starboard tacker's way (rule 43 and definition of an obstruction).

When **Stool-pigeon** calls clearly for room to tack in good time, and white fails to respond, the responsibility is entirely white's and no blame falls on **Stool-pigeon** for white's failure to tack. (As NAYRU case 142 conflicts with IYRU case 6 here, I have taken the IYRU interpretation since, though earlier, it will apply everywhere outside the United States.)

Instead of tacking, **Stool-pigeon** can choose to bear away astern of the starboard boat, since an obstruction can be taken on either side; but she must then give any room white might need if she wishes to go underneath the starboard boat's stern as well (rule 42.1(a) and definition of obstruction).

If white asks for water to bear off behind the starboard boat at the same moment as **Stool-pigeon** asks for room to tack, **Stool-pigeon's** call governs. White only gets room if **Stool-pigeon** choses not to hail for room to tack (NAYRU case 131).

◣◣ Forcing another boat to overstand a weather mark

The team racing ploy of holding an opponent on the same tack to sail beyond the lay line and overstand the weather mark is exactly the same as on a windward leg (page 64).

TACKING

Tacking in the water of a starboard tack boat

A boat which is tacking is required to keep clear of a boat which is not tacking (rule 41). Tacking is explained on page 15.

Even when the tacking boat has completed her tack she is not necessarily in the clear. Any nearby boat on a tack has no need to alter course to avoid her until her tack is complete – that is, until her boom is across and she is sailing on a close-hauled course (though her sails needn't be filling).

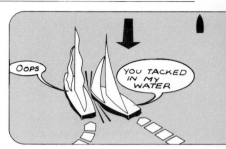

In a protest, the onus is on the boat that tacks to satisfy the race committee that she did so far enough ahead to allow the boat already on the tack to keep clear (rule 41.3 and RYA case 3 1970). In a close tacking incident the boat which is tacking can often help to establish the facts to the satisfaction of a protest committee by calling at the time, 'I'm round now', then counting steadily 1,2,3,4... and stopping when either there's a collision or the other boat overlaps. In spite of the onus of proof, it is possible to tack quite close from port to starboard without breaking any rules.

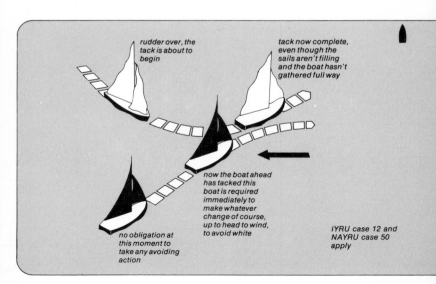

rudder over, the tack is about to begin

tack now complete, even though the sails aren't filling and the boat hasn't gathered full way

now the boat ahead has tacked this boat is required immediately to make whatever change of course, up to head to wind, to avoid white

no obligation at this moment to take any avoiding action

IYRU case 12 and NAYRU case 50 apply

Tacking in the water of a port tack boat

It is not possible to tack as close to another boat when going from starboard tack to port as it is in going from port to starboard.

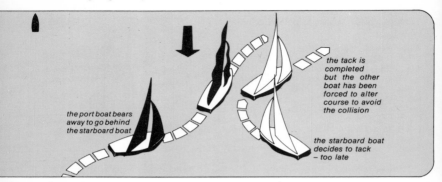

the tack is completed but the other boat has been forced to alter course to avoid the collision

the port boat bears away to go behind the starboard boat

the starboard boat decides to tack – too late

White is in the wrong under rule 35 –which is the one that bars a right-of-way boat from altering course when a give way boat is sailing a course to keep clear. For white to be in the wrong here under rule 35 a protest committee must establish that the port tack boat (black) began to bear off to go behind white before white had begun to tack – that is, before she had passed head to wind.

Once black has borne off, the situation is treated as a close-hauled boat (white) tacking in front of a close reaching boat (black) and the tacking in water rule (41) applies.

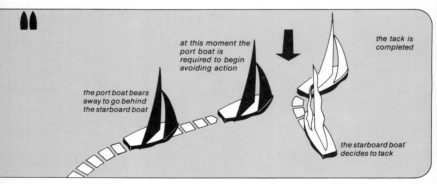

at this moment the port boat is required to begin avoiding action

the tack is completed

the port boat bears away to go behind the starboard boat

the starboard boat decides to tack

At the moment white's tack is completed, black must take whatever avoiding action, including going head to wind, necessary to avoid white. In practice, the port tack boat would head up back to close-hauled as soon as the other boat was seen to be tacking; but for the purposes of deciding a case like this in protest, premature avoiding action by black would not automatically exonerate the tacking boat (rule 41.3).

Simultaneous tacking

When two boats are tacking at the same time, the one on the other's port side keeps clear (rule 41.4).

The easy way to remember simultaneous tacking or gybing onus is quoted in *Elvström Explains* – 'If you're on the right, you're in the right'.

The rule does allow black's helmsman to wait for the other boat's helm to go down and then put his own down, since tacking only happens from the moment a boat goes past head to wind until she is pointing on the new close-hauled course. This takes a little time. As long as the tacking of each boat coincides, they are defined as tacking simultaneously (NAYRU case 129). It is therefore very risky to tack immediately after crossing close ahead of a port tack boat–especially if the port tack boat has borne away to miss the starboard tacker's stern, since she'll be moving extra fast into any tack she might make.

MARK ROUNDING

A boat is rounding a mark from the moment her bow is entering an imaginary circle two lengths from the mark until she has passed the mark.

Where the mark-rounding rules come into force

The special rules which apply to rounding marks and obstructions are in Part IV Section C of the IYRU rules. Rules of that section override rules of Section B with which they conflict. For simplicity's sake here I have dealt separately with mark-rounding. Obstructions are dealt with in the sections on windward legs and offwind legs.

The mark-rounding rules come into force on entering an imaginary circle two lengths from a mark and continue to apply until the mark has been rounded or passed (rule 42.3(a)).

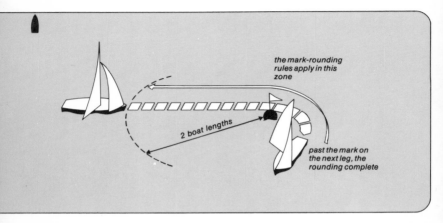

the mark-rounding rules apply in this zone

2 boat lengths

past the mark on the next leg, the rounding complete

A boat overlapped on another which is already in the two lengths circle is also governed by the mark-rounding rules (42.1).

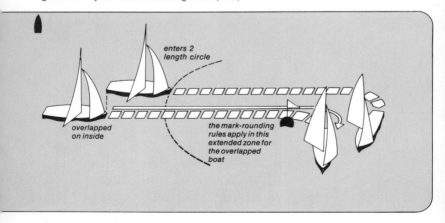

enters 2 length circle

overlapped on inside

the mark-rounding rules apply in this extended zone for the overlapped boat

The zone in which the mark-rounding rules apply can extend further back when:

1. Several boats are overlapped
   The outside boats are required to give room as the boats are 'about to round the mark' (rule 42.1). Which may mean giving room well before the two lengths circle.
   or
2. A leading boat is physically incapable of giving room. For example, a multi-hull travelling fast (in boats other than multi-hulls this special provision, rule 42.3(a)(i), is rarely used).

The penalty for hitting a mark

Hitting a mark is exonerated by a penalty re-rounding of that mark unless the sailing instructions say otherwise (they sometimes specify retirement) or unless the boat was wrongly forced onto the mark by another boat; then she can pass the blame on by protesting against whoever it was forced her onto the mark. A helmsman must either take the required penalty or protest after hitting a mark. Otherwise he risks disqualification (rule 52).

Once the boat has begun her re-rounding manoeuvre she carries no rights over other boats until she has finished it. This part of the rule is far too often ignored, sometimes expensively.

A boat is counted as hitting a mark when any part of her hull, crew or equipment touches it. So a neat hand-off or a spinnaker sheet touching a flag on the mark is a touch (rule 52 and definition of a mark). The mark's mooring line or chain is not counted as part of the mark (definition again) – though the crew may not use the mooring line to stop the boat touching the mark (rule 60).

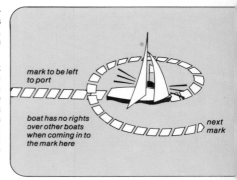

mark to be left
to port

boat has no rights
over other boats
when coming in to
the mark here

next
mark

When a boat hits the 'wrong' side of a mark of the course the penalty re-rounding is more difficult.

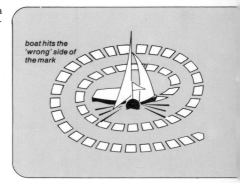

boat hits the
'wrong' side of
the mark

Forced onto a mark by another boat

When a boat is forced onto a mark through, her helmsman believes, a rule infringement by another boat, the helmsman need not take any penalty for hitting the mark provided he protests (rule 52). He can either accept his penalty for hitting the mark and not protest against the other boat, or simply lodge a protest against this other boat. If the protest committee find that the collision with the mark was a result of an infringement by the other boat, the collision with the mark is forgiven and the other boat disqualified. Even when a boat forces you onto a mark and then takes her penalty for the infringement you must still go through the formality of protesting, or you risk being disqualified (rule 52.1).

In the rare event of a mark being submerged by a boat sailing over it, then shooting out of the water to hit a following boat, this boat need not be penalised. She can't protest against the mark, but she can protest against the boat that caused its irregular behaviour (IYRU case 18).

Rights of a boat which has just hit a mark

It can happen that a boat misjudges the course to a mark, hits it and then collides with another boat over which, ignoring the brush with the mark, she would have had right-of-way. What are her rights after touching the mark?

Provided the re-rounding rule is in force (rule 52.2.) she keeps her full rights until 'it is obvious that she is returning to round' the mark and exonerate herself (rule 45.2). So she would be in the right in the incident with the other boat provided she had not obviously begun to return for her re-rounding.

Rounding a mark in the wrong direction

After rounding a mark the wrong way, the mistake can be corrected by unwinding. To do this correctly, a string representing the boat's wake would, when drawn tight, have to lie on the required side of the mark (rule 51.2 and 51.4).

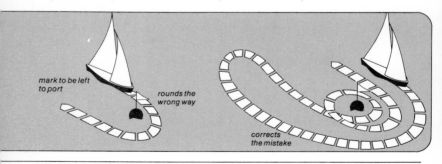

mark to be left to port

rounds the wrong way

corrects the mistake

A mark is only a mark of the course for the leg it defines

A mark is only a mark of the course for a particular boat when it defines the leg of the course which that boat is sailing (rule 52.1(a)(ii)). So on leg 5 - 1 mark 1 is a mark of the course and may not be hit without penalty, but on leg 3 - 4 mark 1 can be hit without penalty.

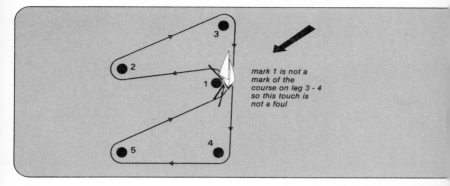

mark 1 is not a
mark of the
course on leg 3 - 4
so this touch is
not a foul

Mark missing or moved

The race committee should return a drifting mark to its stated position if possible. If that isn't possible they must replace it by a new one with 'similar characteristics' or a buoy or boat displaying the letter M of the International Code (rule 9.1(a)). Failing that, the race must be shortened, cancelled, abandoned or postponed (rule 9.1(b)).

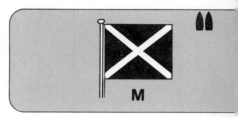

ROUNDING AT THE END OF AN OFFWIND LEG

Room at a mark

A boat which is overlapped on others outside her has the right to room at the mark, provided the overlap is established before the *leading* boat enters an imaginary circle round the mark whose diameter is two of the leading boat's lengths (rules **42.1(a)** and **3(a)(ii)**). The explanation of an **overlap** is on page 16.

If the leading boat is unable to give room, the inside boat is not entitled to it (rule 42.3(a)(i)). In other words she is not expected to do the impossible. Situations in which the leading boat is unable to give room are rare in monohulls but include:

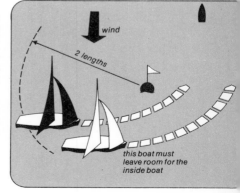

wind

2 lengths

this boat must
leave room for the
inside boat

1. Situations where groups of boats in line abreast simply cannot shift aside fast enough to accommodate a late inside overlapper – even though her overlap may have been established outside the two lengths circle.
2. High speed planing or surfing, when the leading boat just isn't able to respond fast enough two lengths from the mark to let anyone in.

The onus of proof here would almost certainly be with the boat claiming she couldn't give room. Circumstances where a helmsman isn't able to give room because he isn't properly in control of his boat are not included: a helmsman's incompetence or inexperience is no defence (RYA case 4 1975).

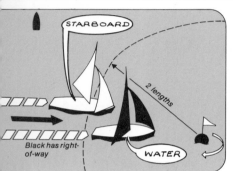

Port and starboard at an offwind mark

The rights of the inside boat take preference over the port and starboard rights, as the note under Section C of the rule book (Part IV) makes clear: 'When a rule of this section applies ... it overrides any conflicting rule of Part IV which precedes it'. The port and starboard rule precedes it.

Before the leader enters the two lengths circle, of course, the starboard boat (white) has right-of-way (rule 36).

The onus in establishing an overlap

A boat which comes from clear astern to claim an inside overlap has the onus of satisfying a protest committee (if the argument gets that far) that the overlap was established in proper time (rule 42.3(d)).

Pusher would find it very difficult to establish that her inside overlap was made soon enough. A witness in another boat or ashore might clinch it, but even so **Pusher** would be foolish in this situation to round on the inside and risk near-certain disqualification. If the outside boat readily concedes the overlap, that's a different matter; then **Pusher** is entitled to round inside.

The onus in breaking an overlap

When two overlapped boats are approaching a mark and just before entering the two lengths circle the outside one claims that she has broken the overlap, she has the onus of satisfying any protest committee that she had become clear ahead before the two lengths circle (**rule 42.3(e)**).

If the inside boat – which doesn't have the onus of proof – strongly disputes a marginal 'clear ahead' claim at the time, the outside helmsman would be stupid to try and push his luck by going for the inside berth.

The onus of proof that the overlap has been broken is on **Quicksilver**, who would be foolish to go for the inside berth unless she could be sure **Barnacle Bill** would not have to avoid her during the rounding.

Hailing for water

The rules don't insist on a hail from the inside boat, but a hail at the time the overlap is either established or ended helps to support the claim (**rule 34.2**). An overlap which is established well before the two lengths circle and is not marginal needs no hail for water from the inside boat.

How overlaps operate when boats are making a wide rounding

In a big fleet it often happens at a leeward mark that boats round very wide at the end of a downwind leg so that they come in close to the mark for a good start to the following leg. If a boat goes so wide that she enters the two lengths circle at right angles to the oncoming fleet, the whole fleet is entitled to water–they are forward of the line at right angles to her aftermost point. They won't all be able to claim water, but some might be able to, as **Interloper** can on the white boat.

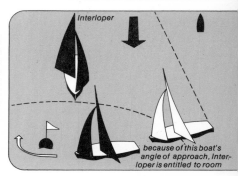

because of this boat's angle of approach, Interloper is entitled to room

▲▲ How overlaps operate when a boat is carried past a mark by a tide

A boat which enters the two lengths circle and leaves it has to establish her overlap rights anew when she re-enters the circle (IRYU case 71).

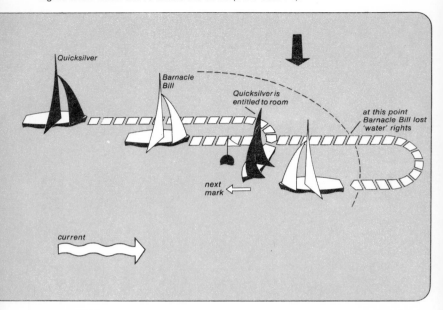

The same principle applies in really windy conditions when a skipper chooses to tack round instead of gybe and during his tack sails past the mark and outside the two lengths circle. He must re-establish new rights on re-entering the circle.

▲ Tacking at a mark

When a tack is an integral part of the rounding – as, say, from a reach to a reach – the rules that apply are exactly the same as in the section on rounding at the end of windward legs (**page 62**). When a boat tacks instead of gybes because it's a bit windy, the tacking in water rules still apply and the overlap conditions are identical to those explained in the section immediately above.

▲ How much room an inside boat is allowed

An inside boat with another overlapped outside her is not entitled to round as wide as she likes within the two lengths circle. To quote IYRU appeal case 40, 'The word "room" in rule 42.1(a) means the room needed by an inside yacht which, in the prevailing conditions, is handled in a seamanlike manner, to pass in safety between an outside yacht and a mark or obstruction'.

This definition makes white's rounding here, in which the outside boat is pushed wide for purely tactical reasons, very risky. The dividing line between what is purely a 'seamanlike' rounding and a rounding made primarily for maximum tactical gain is a fine one. The onus of proof here lies with the outside boat to establish that the inside boat has gone unduly wide. In this situation black would win the protest. One and a half lengths here is too wide; one length would probably not be.

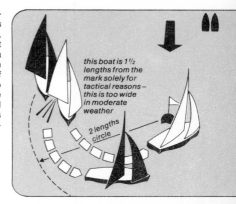

this boat is 1½ lengths from the mark solely for tactical reasons – this is too wide in moderate weather

2 lengths circle

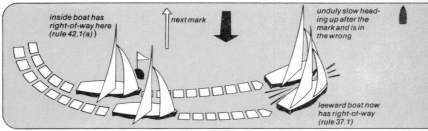

inside boat has right-of-way here (rule 42.1(a))

next mark

unduly slow heading up after the mark and is in the wrong

leeward boat now has right-of-way (rule 37.1)

Once the mark has been passed, the inside boat's rights under the mark-rounding rules end and the right-of-way rules that apply for a leg of the course come into play (IYRU case 50).

Breaking an overlap inside the two lengths circle

An outside boat which is required to give room because of an overlap made before entering the two lengths circle is still required to give room if the overlap is subsequently broken (rule 42.3(c)).

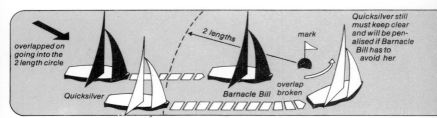

overlapped on going into the 2 length circle

2 lengths

mark

Quicksilver still must keep clear and will be penalised if Barnacle Bill has to avoid her

Quicksilver

Barnacle Bill

overlap broken

Gybing at a mark

There is no such infringement as gybing in someone's water at a mark after starting (rule 42.2(b)).

Inside boat required to gybe at the first opportunity

An inside boat must gybe at the first reasonable opportunity when a gybe is necessary to get on to the proper course for the next leg, except when the inside boat has luffing rights (rule 42.1(b)).

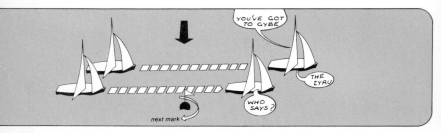

When the inside boat has luffing rights there is no need to get on with the gybe (rule 42.1(b) does not now apply; rule 38.1 does).

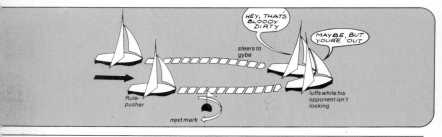

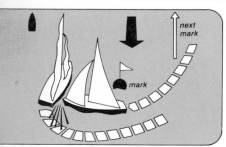

Rounding onto a beat

The port tack boat is in the wrong here, in spite of the right-of-way starboard tack boat altering course. The rule which forbids alteration of course in a way that prevents another boat keeping clear (rule 35) specifically makes an exception of a right-of-way boat rounding a mark. The port and starboard rule (36) governs (NAYRU case 167).

Luffing another boat the wrong side of a mark

This is a curious one which is decidedly not for the newcomer to racing – nor indeed for many old-comers either. But the manoeuvre can work as a defensive move when the helmsman employing the move knows exactly what he's doing and:

1. the rest of the fleet is miles away *or*
2. he's in a team race or match race.

If the manoeuvre is tried when these conditions are not fulfilled all kinds of problems can be expected.

Rule 42.1**(d)** allows an outside boat with luffing rights (**Prima Donna** below) to take an outside boat (**Who Me?**) to windward of a mark provided she warns what she intends to do by hailing, and starts to luff before she is within two lengths of the mark, and provided she also passes to windward of the mark.

This is what the manoeuvre looks like when all goes well:

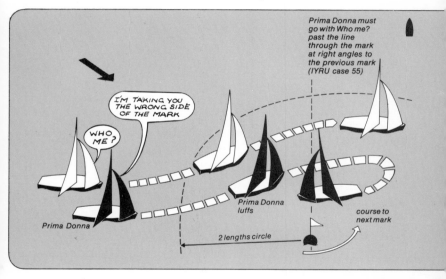

Prima Donna must go with Who me? past the line through the mark at right angles to the previous mark (IYRU case 55)

I'M TAKING YOU THE WRONG SIDE OF THE MARK

WHO ME?

Prima Donna

Prima Donna luffs

2 lengths circle

course to next mark

If the boat (**Who Me?**) being sailed the wrong side of the mark tacks or falls clear **astern** before **Prima Donna** has passed the mark, then **Prima Donna** is entitled to dip **back** and round the mark without first passing the wrong side (IYRU case 61).

The situation I have described here has both boats heading for the mark and about to round up to the moment of the hail and the luff. But when the boat doing the luffing begins the manoeuvre before the boats are about to round the mark – that is, when well clear of the two lengths circle – no hail is necessary. **Prima Donna** could, for example, begin her luff ten lengths from the mark without saying anything and take **Who Me?** well to windward of the mark and beyond without infringing any rule (RYA case 6 1972, NAYRU case 145 and IYRU case 60).

This whole operation is quite involved and must rank favourite for the 'ratio of protests to number of times employed' trophy.

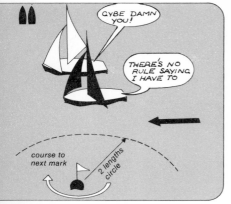

Using starboard rights to sail a boat the wrong side of a mark

When two boats are on opposite tacks the starboard boat may sail above her proper course and the port boat must keep clear (rule 36 and IYRU case **17**). This means that provided both boats remain well outside the two lengths circle the starboard boat may sail the port boat the wrong side of the mark. No hail is necessary in this case, but any necessary alteration of course by the starboard tack boat must be slow to avoid infringing rule 35.

Rounding a mark in opposite directions

When boats are rounding a mark in opposite directions the port and starboard rule (36) applies, no matter whether the starboard boat is rounding the wrong way (IYRU case 37). Of course, if either boat were doing a penalty re-rounding then this boat would have to give way (rule 45.1).

ROUNDING AT THE END OF A WINDWARD LEG

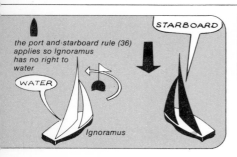

On opposite tacks — port and starboard

When boats on opposite tacks are about to round a windward mark the rules apply essentially as though there were no mark there (rule 42.1(c)).

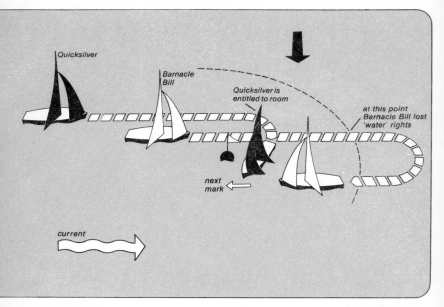

Stopping a luff

A leeward helmsman must stop luffing a windward boat when any of the four following cases apply:

1. He is given a 'mast abeam' call by the windward helmsman. If he doesn't like the call he can protest, but he must respond to it nevertheless. In a dispute over a call the onus lies with the leeward boat to establish that the call was improper. For a 'mast abeam' call by the windward helmsman to be valid, the windward boat must be sailing no higher than the leeward one (rule 38.2). The call is important because without it the leeward helmsman can luff so long as there is doubt about whether the 'mast abeam' position has been reached.
2. There is no doubt that the 'mast abeam' position has been passed (even if there is no call).
3. His boat reaches head to wind. It is not always easy to judge when a boat is head to wind, but a boat may not necessarily have passed head to wind even though her jib has gone aback.
4. The windward helmsman is prevented from responding by an obstruction and calls for room on the obstruction (rule 38.5 and 42.1(a)). Obstructions on which it is possible to make a legitimate 'water' call are dealt with in the definitions on page 17.

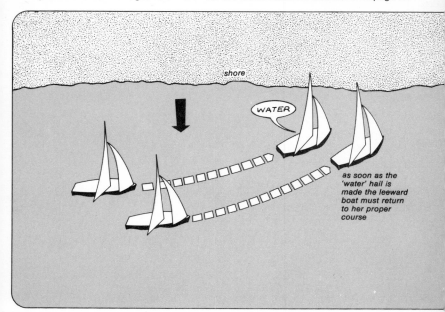

shore

WATER

as soon as the 'water' hail is made the leeward boat must return to her proper course

Once a luff has been stopped by the windward boat the leeward boat must bear away to her proper course (rule 38.1 and 5) – that is, the proper course from the point at which the luff ends, not the course that was proper before the luff started – even if she has to gybe to do so (IYRU case 63).

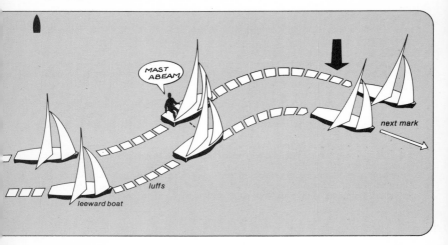

The leeward helmsman is required to respond to the hail immediately. If he does, and there is a collision – even between his tiller extension and the windward boat – the windward boat is in the wrong. But when the leeward boat has to gybe to take up her proper course the original leeward boat will be in the wrong if the collision happens while she is actually gybing,(RYA case 7 1975). The leeward boat must therefore bear away and gybe quickly to keep out of trouble.

When a leeward helmsman refuses to bear off in response to a legitimate 'mast abeam' hail and the windward helmsman gets upset and collides by bearing away to his proper course, both boats are in the wrong: the leeward boat for not responding to the hail, the windward boat for not keeping clear (NAYRU case 15).

Sailing above a proper course without luffing rights

A leeward boat which does not have luffing rights over a windward boat is not entitled to sail above her proper course to the next mark (rule 38.2).

When the windward boat argues that the leeward boat is sailing above her proper course the onus is on the windward boat to prove her case. The leeward boat must be given the benefit of any doubt (IYRU case 25).

When the leeward boat has to gybe to fulfil her obligation not to sail above her proper course she must gybe (IYRU case 63).

However, when a leeward boat refuses to go onto her proper course the windward boat is not entitled to bear off and cause a collision – even when the leeward boat is clearly sailing above her proper course. The leeward boat is certainly luffing illegally, but that does not entitle the windward boat to sail into her and cause a collision. If that happens both boats will be in the wrong – the leeward boat for sailing above her proper course, the windward boat for not keeping clear (NAYRU appeal 15).

GYBING

A boat which is gybing keeps clear

A boat which is gybing is required to keep clear of a boat which isn't (rule 41.1).

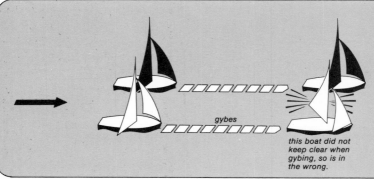

gybes

this boat did not keep clear when gybing, so is in the wrong.

Simultaneous gybing

When two boats are both gybing at the same time the one on the other's port side keeps clear (rule 41.4). The easy way to remember simultaneous gybing and tacking onus is quoted in *Elvström Explains* – 'If you're on the right, you're in the right'.

WHO'S WRONG ?

both gybe

YOU ARE

THE FINISH

The finish ends racing; it is also the beginning of the protest period – when this book may be useful.

▲ Finishing

A boat finishes when any part of her hull or equipment in normal position crosses the finish line (definition) after fulfilling any penalty obligations (that is, re-rounding the finishing mark or carrying out a 720 degree turn).

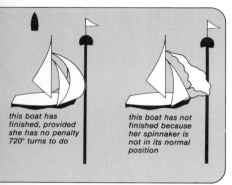

this boat has finished, provided she has no penalty 720° turns to do

this boat has not finished because her spinnaker is not in its normal position

A boat which has finished is still racing until she has cleared the finish line, so a boat which infringes a rule before she has cleared the finish line, but after she has finished, must take her penalty for the infringement.

In the incident below, the port tack boat (white) would not have been penalised if she had been clear of the finish line – that is, no longer intersecting any part of it – since she would not have been racing. Neither boat would then have been penalised (NAYRU case 99).

To clear the finish line it is not necessary to sail right across it. The boat below has finished and cleared the line quite legitimately (rule 51.3 and 5).

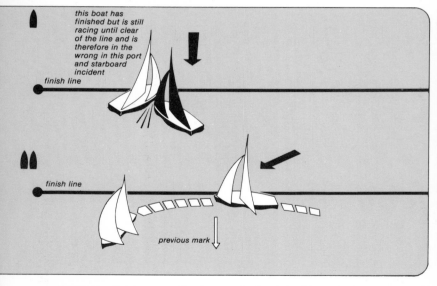

this boat has finished but is still racing until clear of the line and is therefore in the wrong in this port and starboard incident

finish line

finish line

previous mark

A boat also finishes correctly when capsized and the tide carries her across the finish line – provided all the crew are with the boat (IYRU case 1). But the crew may not swim the capsized boat to the finish line (rule 60).

Hitting a finishing mark

Hitting a finishing mark without having cleared the finish line is exonerated by a penalty re-rounding, and the finishing position is counted from the moment the first part of the boat, crew or equipment crosses the finish line the second time. The penalty re-rounding at the port end is to be made anti-clockwise, and at the starboard end clockwise.

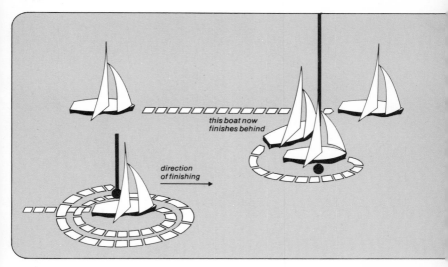

this boat now finishes behind

direction of finishing

If a helmsman is daft enough to hit the wrong side of the finishing mark the re-rounding is more complicated, as you can see on the left.

When a boat has crossed and clears the finish line then hits a finishing mark she is not penalised for the collision because she is no longer racing (definition). The right-of-way rules only apply to boats which are racing (RYA case 8 1975 and NAYRU case 136).

Finish lines

Hook finishes of the kind shown here cannot be enforced by the sailing instructions. Sailing instructions may only override parts of Sections II and III.

They don't override the definition of finishing, which says that a boat finishes when she 'crosses the finish line from the direction of the course from the last mark' –which is clearly the opposite direction to that shown in my diagram, since the last mark is taken to be the last turning mark and not a mark used as a finishing mark (IYRU case 22 and NAYRU case 84).

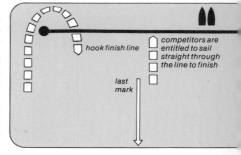

hook finish line

competitors are entitled to sail straight through the line to finish

last mark

OTHER IMPORTANT SAILING RULES, ENFORCEMENT AND PENALTIES

Competitive sailors are their own umpires. If we want rules in our racing, every one of us has an interest in taking our penalties when we ourselves break rules and protesting when someone else does. Otherwise, anarchy.

OTHER IMPORTANT SAILING RULES

▲ Rights of a boat anchored

A boat which is anchored has right-of-way over one which is not. However, an anchored boat must let any boats liable to foul her know that she is at anchor. When two boats are anchored close to one another, the one which anchored last keeps clear, except that a boat dragging keeps clear of one that is not (rule 46).

Anchoring includes lowerng any weight to the bottom, or the crew standing on the bottom holding onto the boat. Anchoring does not mean tying up to or holding onto a mooring, moored boat or jetty. Nor does it mean standing on a jetty to hold the boat (rule 62).

▲ Rights of a boat capsized or aground

A capsized or grounded boat is still racing (rule 46.1), but is not penalised for a collision with another boat. Nor is the other boat penalised if the grounding or capsize happens immediately in front of her (rule 46.3). However, a boat aground must tell any boats which might foul her that she is aground. This is one of only three situations where a collision between two boats racing does not necessarily mean that a protest committee has to disqualify someone (rules 46.1 and 2). One is when a boat has just capsized; another is...

▲ Assisting a boat in distress

There is no penalty for fouling a boat in distress when trying to help (rule 46.3). A boat may have any disadvantage she suffers in assisting a boat in distress rectified (rule 12 explained on page 90).

▲ The contact rule

This rule (33.2) was brought in to tighten up rule observance by placing an onus on people to protest after a collision. Paragraph 1 says: 'When there is contact between the hull, or crew of two yachts, both shall be disqualified unless one of them retires in acknowledgement of an infringement of the rules, or one of both of them acts in accordance with rule 68.3, (Protests).'

Notice that both boats may be disqualified under this rule for any kind of contact, so when a boom of one boat collides with a sail of the other, both boats would be disqualified under rule 33.2 on protest if neither had protested or taken an appropriate penalty.

A third boat which protests that two others collided and that neither took their penalties nor flew protest flags is herself required to fly a protest flag (rule 33 has no clause relieving her of this obligation). But when the two boats come ashore and no protest is lodged, although a protest flag was flown, a third helmsman witnessing the collision may then lodge a protest, even after the normal time limit has expired (rule 68.3(b)).

When a race committee knows of a collision which did not result in a protest or voluntary penalty they may call a protest hearing of both boats involved (rule 73.2(a),(b),(d) and the final paragraph of the rule). The race committee are not *obliged* to act under rule 73 (although they must if a protest is properly lodged on the same incident by a competitor). Even if the collision happened right in front of the race officer they need do nothing, though in that case they would be wise to act.

But if they do decide to act, any protest brought under this rule must be given a formal hearing. The boats cannot be summarily disqualified on the say-so of a witness to the collision, even if he's the race officer.

When contact between two boats is minor and neither takes a penalty or protests, the protest committee is entitled to disqualify only one of the boats on protest, not both as they would have to do if the collision where not minor (rule 33.3). Minor contact is often unavoidable on start lines.

Fair sailing

The fair sailing rule is designed to catch people who have done something naughty which has somehow not been covered by the complex net of the main rules. It only applies when no other rule can be invoked. So any protest hearing in which the fair sailing rule is used must be long if the case is to be properly considered: the protest committee are required to scour the rule book for any other rule which might apply instead. The rule is the first in the book.

Unfair sailing is one of those terms which cannot be precisely defined, since what is unfair to one sailor may be perfectly fair and all part of the game to another. This rule has tended, recently, to be used to catch out people whose ingenuity has lent itself to novel ways of disqualifying opponents. Intent is important here. A boat was disqualified when her crew deliberately stretched out an arm to hit a windward boat which was keeping clear (RYA case 6 1971). Another was disqualified for deliberately heeling the boat to windward so that the mast would collide with an overtaking windward boat (RYA case 9 1969).   (This rule is used extremely rarely.)

Illegal propulsion

'A yacht shall be propelled only by the natural action of the wind on the sails, spars and hull, and water on the hull, and shall not check way be abnormal means...' (rule 60.1).

There are several exceptions to this principle, three of them rare, one common. The rare ones are: a boat may be propelled by paddling or other 'abnormal' means when recovering someone overboard or when rendering assistance (rules 60.1 and 58), and may be pulled afloat after grounding by first rowing an anchor out in a boat.

The common exception is to use sharp sail and body movements to help propel a boat. These are legitimate under certain conditions (rule 60.2 and Appendix 2). A careful reading of the Appendix makes it fairly clear what is and what is not allowed. Roll tacks and roll gybes are allowed, so long as they are not unduly frequent, when they would be regarded as illegal propulsion. Many roll tackers have been disqualified on protest under rule 60.

Repeated trimming and releasing of sails is allowed only in surfing or planing conditions and then only to make the boat begin planing or surfing. When surfing down a wave, repeated pumping is not legitimate. The rule applies to all sails, not just mainsails.

In some single-handed classes and light displacement two-handers this rule is widely abused. Race committees can do a lot to enforce the rule by bringing protests against alleged offenders (rule 73.2).

Alternatively they may specify in their sailing instructions an experimental pumping and ooching rule (60.3) which allows complete freedom to pump and ooch when a specified signal is given. A second signal, which must also be specified in the sailing instructions, is given at the next turning mark and the experimental rules ceases to apply.

Braking

A boat's way must not be checked by 'abnormal means' (rule 60). These include holding a bucket over the side, putting an arm or leg in the water or fitting water brakes. Back-winding sails is regarded as 'the natural action of wind on the sails', to quote the rule, and is allowed (NAYRU case 132).

PENALTIES AND RULE ENFORCEMENT

Disqualification and retirement

A boat which is found by a protest committee to have infringed a rule or a sailing instruction is disqualified from the race in which the infringement happened. An exception is a boat that retired promptly after the incident, but still protested the other boat: if she lost the protest she would not be disqualified but would be counted as having retired (rule 31.1).

Retirement for a rule infringement has to happen promptly after the incident or the retiring boat may be disqualified (rule 33.1). Promptly does not mean immediately. A reasonable time is allowed to work out whether to retire, protest or do nothing. Two minutes may be too short a time to reach a decision; five minutes I would say is usually too long.

If the sailing instructions specify one of the alternative penalty systems, special penalties apply to any boat which infringes a rule of Part IV (the right-of-way rules). The two alternative penalty systems are the 720 degree turns and the percentage rule.

Alternative penalties (Appendix 3)

The standards of rule observance have fallen in recent years. This is partly attributable to a widespread feeling, expressed by a refusal to retire after infringing a rule or to protest against other wrong-doers, that retirement from a race is too harsh a penalty for breaking a rule. The alternative penalty systems were introduced to make it easier for people to acknowledge their errors by paying a lesser price. And generally the systems work well. The 720 degree penalty works best for one design boats, especially the smaller ones, and is explained below. The percentage penalties work best for offshore racing and larger boats. The special appendix that deals with percentage penalties is self explanatory.

Alternative penalties apply only to infringements of rules in Part IV (the right-of-way rules), and use of either system must be specified in the sailing instructions, otherwise retirement and disqualification are in force (rule 3.2(b)(xiv)).

720 degree turns (Appendix 3)

A boat which breaks a rule of Part IV may exonerate herself by making two full 360 degree turns, during which she has no rights over any other boats. She may then carry on with the race.

If she does not acknowledge her error, she may be disqualified after a protest (under rule 68) by another boat or by the race committee (rule 73.2) Appendix 3, clause 1.6).

The boat which is fouled has to hail the wrongdoer that she intends to protest. The wrongdoer must then do her turns at the first reasonable opportunity (clause 1.1). This usually means as soon as she can work into a clear enough patch of water to gyrate without colliding with other boats, and that may sometimes be on the following leg (clause 1.2 does not say 'same leg'). Clear water must be sought; it is not good enough to sail on for five minutes waiting for a space to appear.

The turns must both be done in the same direction, one immediately after the other, and must be full turns. That means that on windward leg a helmsman may not go into his turns from close-hauled starboard and leave them close-hauled on port as often happens (clause 1.3).

Before the starting signal, the infringing boat must wait till after the starting signal has gone, then do her turns as soon as she can. If the turns are not properly done, the

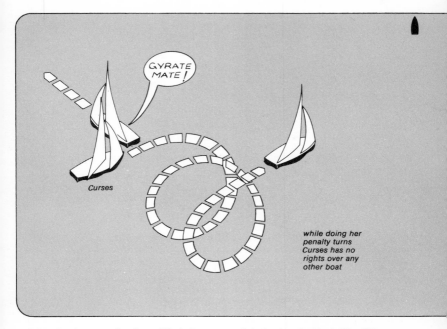

GYRATE MATE!

Curses

while doing her penalty turns Curses has no rights over any other boat

infringing boat may be disqualified after a properly lodged protest (rule 68 or 73).

When serious damage is caused in a collision either boat may be disqualified, even when the turns have been properly done (clause 1.8).

It is possible under the 720 degree rule for a helmsman very occasionally to deliberately infringe a rule, do the turns and end up better off after the incident than he would have by obeying the rules. A boat beating to a windward mark, for example, against a strong tide in light air might lose less ground by refusing to give way to a starboard boat and take the penalty turns after rounding the mark than by tacking for the starboard boat and failing to lay the mark.

The port boat then could be disqualified on protest (Appendix 3, clause 1.9 and rules 68 or 73), even though she might have done her turns immediately after the incident.

After a collision and when the turns aren't properly carried out – either through some technicality or only one turn being done – the right-of-way boat is protected by clause 1.7 of Appendix 3 from being disqualified under rule 35.2 (Contact between yachts, explained on page 84).

Penalty points in team racing

In team racing a penalty points system is now widely used. A helmsman who infringes a rules and acknowledges his infringement continues racing and takes a 3 point penalty. If he infringes a second or third time in that race, he takes another 3 point penalty for each infringement he acknowledges. A lost protest costs him 5 points or in some competitions 6 points, depending on what the sailing instructions specify.

An acknowledged infringement is signalled by tying a green flag to the shroud and a protest is signalled by tying on a red flag. Once a helmsman flies a green flag he may not take it down and fly a red one to protest over the incident. But if he first puts up a red one with the intention of protesting, then thinks better of it, he may take it down and fly the green one – provided the switch happens promptly after the incident.

The advantage of this system is that the balance of a team race is not destroyed either by losing a boat from one team or by the excessive points penalty of a well-placed boat being disqualified. Its provisions must be stated clearly in the sailing instructions. The 720 degree penalty has also been found to work well in team races.

The penalty for not protesting

After a collision with another boat, failure to protest may mean disqualification. If the other boat doesn't protest, either a third boat or anyone else who saw the incident may have both boats disqualified after a protest hearing (rule 33.2, explained on page 84).

When a rule infringement does not result in a collision there is little risk of disqualification in failing to lodge a protest.

A boat which hits a mark must either retire (or re-round when the re-rounding rule operates) or protest – even if she was forced onto the mark and the boat that forced her onto the mark took the penalty for the infringement (rule 52.1(b)). So if you are forced onto a mark always protest, re-round it or retire.

Making the rules work

There can be no effective umpires or referees in sailing as there are in games like football and cricket. With sometimes over a hundred competitors but no ball to blaze a trail of fouls, the practical difficulties of even seeing fouls on the water are enormous. To make matters worse, the complexity of the present sailing rules would make any instant decisions by a referee extremely unreliable. We sailors are therefore our own umpires. When people foul us and don't take their voluntary penalty we should protest; when we break a rule we should take our penalty voluntarily.

In a fleet where nobody ever protests or retires, the rules cease to exist. The racing is then decidedly less satisfactory than when behaviour on the water is controlled – at least approximately – by a known code, the IYRU rules.

Protest by one competitor against another

When a helmsman thinks he has been fouled by another boat – whether there is a collision or not – or when he thinks any other competitor has broken a rule or infringed one of the sailing instructions, he is entitled to protest (rule 68.1). A protest is decided ashore by a protest committee, which is a sub-committee of the race committee. It acts in much the same way as a court of law, first hearing the evidence and then giving its verdict as to which boats, if any, are disqualified.

A helmsman who decides to protest must fly a protest flag (rule 68.3). Code flag B is always acceptable, and in racing governed by the North American Yacht Racing Union a broad interpretation of a protest flag is acceptable. In one case a piece of red cellophane was allowed (NAYRU case 88). Variations on code flag B in races under the Royal Yachting Association's control are limited to a piece of rectangular material no smaller than the boat's burgee or distinguishing flag (RYA prescription).

A protest flag must be flown in the rigging, except in a singlehander where it may be waved by the protesting helmsman soon after the incident and waved again on finishing.

A protest committee is only allowed to hear a protest for which no flag was flown when:

1. The facts of the incident were not known until after the finish – for example, when a boat is alleged to have touched another and her crew was unaware of any collision

at the time. But ignorance of a rule interpretation or a sailing instruction does not rate as a reason for failing to fly a protest flag at the time of an incident (rule 68.3(b), IYRU case 47).
2. Protesting about some error or omission of the race committee (rules 12, 68.5(a)).
3. The boat which intends to protest is dismasted (NAYRU case 153).
4. A boat sees a collision between two others and neither of the colliding boats goes through with a protest, although one or both flew flags soon after the incident (rules 33.2 and 68.3(b)).

Otherwise, a protest flag must be flown 'at the first reasonable opportunity' after the incident (rule 68.3(a)).This is vague, but appeal cases have made the intention fairly clear. Two legs after the incident is too late (NAYRU case 174), but the flag must be flown within 'a reasonably short time' of the incident (NAYRU case 3). When a clear statement of the intention to protest is made at the time of the incident, more latitude may be allowed in putting up the flag – although allowing as legitimate a flag which first appeared two miles after the incident (NAYRU case 105) is a unique case and should not be quoted as a precedent. In extremely heavy weather, the 'first reasonable opportunity' in a boat which relies primarily for crew weight on stability may well be after the finish.

'A protesting yacht shall try to inform the yacht protested against that a protest will be lodged' (rule 68.3(c)). The attempt is the important thing. The helmsman protested against need not necessarily have heard the call. Nor is there a time limit on when the call should happen, as there is on putting up a protest flag.

On coming ashore the boat protesting must put in a written protest or at least make a verbal statement to the race committee (rule 68.3(d) and IYRU case 29). The protest must be delivered, or mailed if this is impossible, within two hours of the time the protester finishes, although when a race committee feel that particular circumstances justify them in extending the time limit they may do so (rule 68.3(e)). Sailing instructions often set different time limits which override the standard IYRU ruling.

The defendant is entitled to a copy of the protest. If he asks for it and is not given it, the protest would be dismissed on appeal (NAYRU case 82). If he doesn't ask for it, that would not be grounds on which an appeal would be dismissed (NAYRU case 133).

A cash deposit is still required by some clubs. The deposit is returnable after the protest hearing and serves no useful purpose. The practice of charging a protest fee returnable only to the helmsman who is not disqualified is decidedly not recommended; it discourages protests, which in turn encourages greater rule abuse. If race committees fine well-meaning people for losing protests, who is ever going to protest? And without protests there is no such thing as rule observance.

Protest by a race committee

A race committee can call on its own initiative for a protest hearing to deal with a possible rule infringement by a competitor (rule 73.2). The hearing is carried out as though a protest has been made against the infringing boat by another competitor (rule 73.2(d) and (e)).

A race committee can start its own proceedings in the following circumstances:

1. A member of the race committee may have seen the infringement.
2. The infringement may have been reported the same day by a disinterested non-competitor.
3. The race committee may have had grounds for believing that an infringement resulted in serious damage.
4. A boat involved in a protest may have committed some other infringement (rule 73.2).

But however blatant a competitor's infringement, the race committee is not allowed to disqualify any boat without a formal hearing, provided that the boat started and finished correctly (rule 73.1(a) and the last sentence of 73.2).

Disqualification without a hearing

The only infringements for which a race committee may disqualify a boat without a hearing are failing to start or finish correctly. Even then, a competitor who is disqualified without a hearing is entitled to one if he can bring reasonable evidence that the race committee has made a mistake (rule 73.1(a)).

Protest against the race committee

These are more difficult to win than any others, partly because the protest committee, being a sub-committee of the race committee, is often inclined to regard the point of view of a hard-worked race officer more sympathetically than a trouble-making, self-interested competitor. A good protest committee will guard against this tendency and weigh the evidence as faily as possible

The protest is not strictly against the race committee, but is a plea by a helmsman that his finishing position has been 'materially prejudiced... by an action or omission of the race committee' (rule 12). As the rule is an important one and is not quoted in the back of this book, I will quote it in full.

When:

(a) the race committee, upon its own initiative, decides; or

(b) a yacht seeks redress from the race committee under rule 68.5(a), Protests, within the time limit prescribed by rule 68.3(e); on the grounds that through no fault of the yacht concerned, her finishing position has been materially prejudiced by:

  (i) an action or omission of the race committee; or

  (ii) rendering assistance in accordance with rule 58, Rendering Assistance; or

  (iii) being disabled by another vessel which was required to keep clear; the race committee shall make such arrangement as it deems equitable; which may be to let the results of the race stand; to adjust the points scored or the finishing time of the prejudiced yacht; or to abandon or cancel the race, provided that the race committee shall not act under this rule before satisfying itself by taking appropriate evidence that its action is as equitable as possible to all yachts concerned, for that particular race and for the series, if any, as a whole.

The rule also covers giving assistance to someone in distress while racing, and being disabled by a right-of-way boat. Any doubt about the anticipated finishing position of the boat giving assistance, or disabled, should be resolved in favour of that boat.

The race committee is required to find the least unfair solution; and solutions to be explored rather than resorting to the easy option of cancellation or abandonment include re-arrangements of the finishing order or settling for the order recorded at the mark prior to the incident. A race thrown out is unfair to the people who were up front that day; if there is a different solution which is reasonably fair to everybody, that's the one the committee should go for. If not, the race must be abandoned.

When there is reasonable doubt about whether a competitor was prejudiced, the doubt must be resolved in favour of the competitor (NAYRU case 66). But notice that a competitor's chances of winning a prize must be prejudiced, so if he had no chance of winning a prize, either in that race or the series, before the incident, there is no case to answer.

Composition of a protest committee

A protest committee is appointed by the race committee and is, strictly, part of the race committee. No-one may be on a protest committee who might benefit from that committee's decision. Interpreted strictly, this would bar competitors from protest committees (NAYRU case 124), but in practice competitors can be included provided both protester and defendant agree to it. So at the start of the hearing, the protester and defendant should be asked whether they object to any member of the protest committee, those members who competed in the race or the series being pointed out. If there are no objections, any right of appeal on that score is automatically invalid (NAYRU case 175).

Extra care in the appointment of a protest committee is called for when the protest is, effectively, against the race committee for some error or oversight in the running of a race (rule 12). The race committee is then sitting in judgement on itself through its protest committee. Ideally the protest committee should consist of people who were neither involved in the race as competitors nor as organisers. Then injustice is not seen to be done.

The right to appeal

The final arbiter in a dispute over the IYRU rules is the national sailing authority of the country in which the event is sailed. However, a formal appeal to the national authority can only be considered on questions of rule interpretation, not on questions of fact. The final arbiter of fact is the protest committee in the first place (rule 77).

For some national events, like World Championships, a special jury is appointed which is competent enough for there to be no right of appeal. This waiving of appeal is also common in two day team racing events where teams must be eliminated from early rounds before there can be a final and winners. An appeal on a first round result would dislocate the whole event.

The right to waive appeal is only given by a national or the international sailing authority; it is not given lightly.

Counter-protest

It often happens that both boats involved in an incident lodge a protest. In practice it doesn't matter which protest is actually heard, since only the order of the hearing will be affected. The onus of proof will in no way change. However, if one boat in a collision fails to protest, or fails to fly a protest flag properly, and the other boat withdraws her protest, the boat which fails to lodge a valid protest may not have her protest heard (NAYRU case 49).

The protest hearing

The procedure for hearing a protest is well explained in Appendix 6 of the IYRU rules. It is important to follow this carefully, because a hearing in which there are major errors of procedure may invalidate a protest (NAYRU case 54). But if either the protester or defendant (referred to as 'protestee' in the rule book) feels that procedural errors are being made, these should be pointed out at the time. Failure to complain at the time, or as soon afterwards as the wrong procedure became known, would mean that an appeal based on the procedural errors would be dismissed (NAYRU case 176).

The defendant and the protester have the right to be present at the hearing and throughout the taking of evidence (rule 70.1). When either the defendant or protester has made a reasonable attempt to be present he should be allowed to be present. So if a committee has several protests to hear, it should hear those where both parties are present first (NAYRU case 104). But if an interested party fails to make an effort to be at the hearing, a committee may deal with the case without a full hearing (rule 70.3 and NAYRU case 54).

The protester and defendant may call as many witnesses as they choose (rule 70.1) unless witnesses re-iterate facts that have already been established (NAYRU case 54).

A protest committee will usually put its findings in writing in the form 'facts found:...' and 'decisions:...' quoting the rule numbers that apply. There is no obligation to do it this way though, unless asked to do so (NAYRU case 54). Otherwise it may give its decision verbally (rule 71).

THE 1977 RACING RULES OF THE INTERNATIONAL YACHT RACING UNION

Parts I, IV, V & VI AND APPENDICES 2, 3 & 6

Introduction

Translation and Interpretation
In translating and interpreting these rules, it shall be understood that the word "shall" is mandatory, and the words "can" and "may" are permissive.

Note   No changes are contemplated before 1981.

Fundamental Rule

Fair Sailing

A yacht shall compete in an event only by fair sailing, superior speed and skill, and, except in team races, by individual effort. However, a yacht may be disqualified under this rule only in the case of a clear-cut violation of the above principles and only when no other rule applies.

PART 1 – **Definitions**

When a term defined in Part 1 is used in its defined sense it is printed in *italic* type. All preambles and definitions rank as rules.

Racing – A yacht is *racing* from her preparatory signal until she has either *finished* and cleared the finishing line and finishing *marks* or retired, or until the race has been *postponed*, *abandoned* or *cancelled*, except that in match or team races, the sailing instructions may prescribe that a yacht is *racing* from any specified time before the preparatory signal.

Starting – A yacht *starts* when, after fulfilling her penalty obligations, if any, under rule 51.1(c), (Sailing the Course), and after her starting signal, any part of her hull, crew or equipment first crosses the starting line in the direction of the course to the first *mark*.

Finishing – A yacht *finishes* when any part of her hull, or of her crew or equipment in normal position, crosses the finishing line from the direction of the course from the last *mark*, after fulfilling her penalty obligations, if any, under rule 52.2, (Touching a Mark).

Luffing – Altering course towards the wind until head to wind.

Tacking – A yacht is *tacking* from the moment she is beyond head to wind until she has *borne away*, if beating to windward, to a *close-hauled* course; if not beating to windward, to the course on which her mainsail has filled.

Bearing Away – Altering course away from the wind until a yacht begins to *gybe*.

Gybing – A yacht begins to *gybe* at the moment when, with the wind aft, the foot of her mainsail crosses her centre line, and completes the *gybe* when the mainsail has filled on the other *tack*.

On a Tack – A yacht is *on a tack* except when she is *tacking* or *gybing*. A yacht is on the tack (*starboard* or *port*) corresponding to her *windward* side.

Close-hauled – A yacht is *close-hauled* when sailing by the wind as close as she can lie with advantage in working to windward.

Clear Astern and *Clear Ahead; Overlap* – A yacht is *clear astern* of another when her hull and equipment in normal position are abaft an imaginary line projected abeam from the aftermost point of the other's hull and equipment in normal position. The other yacht is *clear ahead*. The yachts *overlap* if neither is *clear astern* ; or if, although one is *clear astern*, an intervening yacht *overlaps* both of them. The terms *clear astern*, *clear ahead* and *overlap* apply to yachts on opposite *tacks* only when they are subject to rule 42, (Rounding or Passing Marks and Obstructions).

Leeward and *Windward* — The *leeward* side of a yacht is that on which she is, or, if *luffing* head to wind, was, carrying her mainsail. The opposite side is the *windward* side.
When neither of two yachts on the same *tack* is *clear astern*, the one on the *leeward* side of the other is the *leeward yacht*. The other is the *windward yacht*.

Proper Course — A *proper course* is any course which a yacht might sail after the starting signal, in the absence of the other yacht or yachts affected, to *finish* as quickly as possible. The course sailed before *luffing* or *bearing away* is presumably, but not necessarily, that yacht's *proper course*. There is no *proper course* before the starting signal.

Mark — A *mark* is any object specified in the sailing instructions which a yacht must round or pass on a required side.
Every ordinary part of a *mark* ranks as part of it, including a flag, flagpole, boom or hoisted boat, but excluding ground tackle and any object either accidentally or temporarily attached to the *mark*.

Obstruction — An *obstruction* is any object, including a vessel under way, large enough to require a yacht, if not less than one overall length away from it, to make a substantial alteration of course to pass on one side or the other, or any object which can be passed on one side only, including a buoy when the yacht in question cannot safely pass between it and the shoal or object which it marks.

Postponement — A *postponed* race is one which is not started at its scheduled time and which can be sailed at any time the race committee may decide.

Abandonment — An *abandoned* race is one which the race committee declares void at any time after the starting signal, and which can be re-sailed at its discretion.

Cancellation — A *cancelled* race is one which the race committee decides will not be sailed thereafter.

PART IV – **Right of Way Rules**

Rights and Obligations when Yachts Meet

The rules of Part IV do not apply in any way to a vessel which is neither intending to race nor racing ; such vessel shall be treated in accordance with the International Regulations for Preventing Collisions at Sea or Government Right of Way Rules applicable in the area concerned.

The rules of Part IV apply only between yachts which either are intending to *race* or are *racing* in the same or different races, and, except when rule 3.2(b)(ii), (Race Continues After Sunset), applies, replace the International Regulations for Preventing Collisions at Sea or Government Right of Way Rules applicable to the area concerned, from the time a yacht intending to *race* begins to sail about in the vicinity of the starting line until she has either *finished* or retired and has left the vicinity of the course.

SECTION A – **Obligations and Penalties**

31   Disqualification

31.1   A yacht may be disqualified or otherwise penalised for infringing a rule of Part IV only when the infringement occurs while she is *racing*, whether or not a collision results.

31.2   A yacht may be disqualified before or after she is *racing* for seriously hindering a yacht which is *racing*, or for infringing the sailing instructions.

32   Avoiding Collisions

A right-of-way yacht which fails to make a reasonable attempt to avoid a collision resulting in serious damage may be disqualified as well as the other yacht.

33   Rule Infringement

33.1   ACCEPTING PENALTY
A yacht which realises she has infringed a racing rule or a sailing instruction is under an obligation either to retire promptly or to exonerate herself by

accepting an alternative penalty when so prescribed in the sailing instructions, but when she does not retire or exonerate herself and persists in *racing*, other yachts shall continue to accord her such rights as she may have under the rules of Part IV.

33.2   CONTACT BETWEEN YACHTS RACING
When there is contact between the hull, equipment or crew of two yachts, both shall be disqualified or otherwise penalised unless :
either

(a) one of the yachts retires in acknowledgement of the infringement, or exonerates herself by accepting an alternative penalty, when so prescribed in the sailing instructions, or

(b) one or both of the yachts acts in accordance with rule 68.3, (Protests).

33.3   When an incident is the subject of action by the race committee under rule 33.2 but under no other rule of Part IV, it may waive the requirements of rule 33.2 when it is satisfied that the contact was minor and unavoidable.

34   Hailing

34.1   Except when *luffing* under rule 38.1, (Luffing and Sailing above a Proper Course after Starting), a right-of-way yacht which does not hail before or when making an alteration of course which may not be foreseen by the other yacht may be disqualified as well as the yacht required to keep clear when a collision resulting in serious damage occurs.

34.2   A yacht which hails when claiming the establishment or termination of an *overlap* or insufficiency of room at a *mark* or *obstruction* thereby helps to support her claim for the purposes of rule 42, (Rounding or Passing Marks and Obstructions).

SECTION B – **Principal Right of Way Rules and their Limitations**

These rules apply except when over-ridden by a rule in Section C.

35   Limitations on Altering Course

When one yacht is required to keep clear of another, the right-of-way yacht shall not so alter course as to prevent the other yacht from keeping clear ; or so as to obstruct her while she is keeping clear, except :

(a) to the extent permitted by rule 38.1, (Same Tack, Luffing after Starting), and

(b) when assuming a *proper* course :
either

> (i) to *start*, unless subject to rule 40, (Same Tack, Luffing before Starting), or to the second part of rule 44.1 (b), (Returning to Start),

or

> (ii) when rounding a *mark*.

36   Opposite Tacks — Basic Rule

A *port-tack* yacht shall keep clear of a *starboard-tack* yacht.

37   Same Tack — Basic Rules

37.1 WHEN OVERLAPPED
A *windward yacht* shall keep clear of a *leeward yacht*.

37.2 WHEN NOT OVERLAPPED
A yacht *clear astern* shall keep clear of a yacht *clear ahead*.

37.3 TRANSITIONAL
A yacht which establishes an *overlap* to *leeward* from *clear astern* shall allow the *windward yacht* ample room and opportunity to keep clear.

38   Same Tack — Luffing and Sailing above a Proper Course after Starting

38.1 LUFFING RIGHTS
After she has *started* and cleared the starting line, a yacht *clear ahead* or a *leeward yacht* may *luff* as she pleases, subject to the *proper course* limitations of this rule.

38.2 PROPER COURSE LIMITATIONS
A *leeward yacht* shall not sail above her *proper course* while an *overlap* exists, if when the *overlap* began or, at any time during its existence, the helmsman of the *windward yacht* (when sighting abeam from his normal station and sailing no higher than the *leeward yacht*) has been abreast or forward of the mainmast of the *leeward yacht*.

38.3 OVERLAP LIMITATIONS
For the purpose of this rule : An *overlap* does not exist unless the yachts are clearly within two overall lengths of the longer yacht ; and an *overlap* which exists between two yachts when the leading yacht *starts*, or when one or both of them completes a *tack* or *gybe*, shall be regarded as a new *overlap* beginning at that time.

38.4 HAILING TO STOP OR PREVENT A LUFF
When there is doubt, the *leeward yacht* may assume that she has the right to *luff* unless the helmsman of the *windward yacht* has hailed "Mast Abeam",

or words to that effect. The *leeward yacht* shall be governed by such hail, and, if she deems it improper, her only remedy is to protest.

38.5 CURTAILING A LUFF
The *windward yacht* shall not cause a *luff* to be curtailed because of her proximity to the *leeward yacht* unless an *obstruction*, a third yacht or other object restricts her ability to respond.

38.6 LUFFING TWO OR MORE YACHTS
A yacht shall not *luff* unless she has the right to *luff* all yachts which would be affected by her *luff*, in which case they shall all respond even if an intervening yacht or yachts would not otherwise have the right to *luff*.

39 Same Tack – Sailing Below a Proper Course after Starting

A yacht which is on a free leg of the course shall not sail below her *proper course* when she is clearly within three of her overall lengths of either a *leeward yacht* or a yacht *clear astern* which is steering a course to pass to *leeward*.

40 Same Tack – Luffing before Starting

Before a right-of-way yacht has *started* and cleared the starting line, any *luff* on her part which causes another yacht to have to alter course to avoid a collision shall be carried out slowly and in such a way as to give a *windward yacht* room and opportunity to keep clear, but the *leeward yacht* shall not so *luff* above a *close-hauled* course, unless the helmsman of the *windward yacht* (sighting abeam from his normal station) is abaft the mainmast of the *leeward yacht*. Rules 38.4, (Hailing to Stop or Prevent a Luff) ; 38.5, (Curtailing a Luff) ; and 38.6, (Luffing Two or more Yachts), also apply.

41 Changing Tack – Tacking and Gybing

41.1 BASIC RULE
A yacht which is either *tacking* or *gybing* shall keep clear of a yacht on *a tack*.

41.2 TRANSITIONAL
A yacht shall neither *tack* nor *gybe* into a position which will give her right of way unless she does so far enough from a yacht *on a tack* to enable this yacht to keep clear without having to begin to alter her course until after the *tack* or *gybe* has been completed.

41.3 ONUS
A yacht which *tacks* or *gybes* has the onus of satisfying the race committee that she completed her *tack* or *gybe* in accordance with rule 41.2.

41.4 WHEN SIMULTANEOUS
When two yachts are both *tacking* or both *gybing* at the same time, the one on the other's *port* side shall keep clear.

SECTION C – **Rules which apply at marks and obstructions and other exceptions to the Rules of Section B**

When a rule of this section applies, to the extent to which it explicitly provides rights and obligations, it over-rides any conflicing rule of Section B, Principal Right of Way Rules and their Limitations except rule 35, (Limitations on Altering Course).

42 **Rounding or Passing Marks and Obstructions**

42.1 ROOM AT MARKS AND OBSTRUCTIONS WHEN OVERLAPPED
When yachts are about to round or pass a *mark*, other than a starting *mark* surrounded by navigable water, on the same required side or an *obstruction* on the same side :

(a) An outside yacht shall give each yacht *overlapping* her on the inside, room to round or pass the *mark* or *obstruction*, except as provided in rules 42.1(c), 42.1(d) and 42.4, (At a Starting Mark Surrounded by Navigable Water). Room includes room for an *overlapping* yacht to *tack* or *gybe* when either is an integral part of the rounding or passing manoeuvre.

(b) When an inside yacht of two or more *overlapped* yachts either on opposite *tacks*, or on the same *tack* without *luffing* rights, will have to *gybe* in order most directly to assume a *proper course* to the next *mark*, she shall *gybe* at the first reasonable opportunity.

(c) When two yachts on opposite *tacks* are on a beat or when one of them will have to *tack* either to round the *mark* or to avoid the *obstruction*, as between each other rule 42.1 shall not apply and they are subject to rules 36, (Opposite Tacks Basic Rule), and 41, (Changing Tack – Tacking or Gybing).

(d) An outside *leeward yacht* with luffing rights may take an inside yacht to windward of a *mark* provided that she hails to that effect and begins to *luff* before she is within two of her overall lengths of the *mark* and provided that she also passes to windward of it.

42.2 CLEAR ASTERN AND CLEAR AHEAD IN THE VICINITY OF MARKS AND OB-STRUCTIONS
When yachts are about to round or pass a *mark*, other than a starting *mark* surrounded by navigable water, on the same required side or an *obstruction* on the same side :

(a) A yacht *clear astern* shall keep clear in anticipation of and during the rounding or passing manoeuvre when the yacht *clear ahead* remains on the same *tack* or *gybes*.

(b) A yacht *clear ahead* which *tacks* to round a *mark* is subject to rule 41, (Changing Tack – Tacking or Gybing), but a yacht *clear astern* shall not *luff* above *close-hauled* so as to prevent the yacht *clear ahead* from *tacking*.

42.3 LIMITATIONS ON ESTABLISHING AND MAINTAINING AN OVERLAP IN THE VICINITY OF MARKS AND OBSTRUCTIONS
(a) A yacht *clear astern* may establish an inside *overlap* and be entitled to room under rule 42.1, (Room at Marks and Obstructions when Yachts are Overlapped), only when the yacht *clear ahead*:

(i) is able to give the required room and

(ii) is outside two of her overall lengths of the *mark* or *obstruction*, except when either yacht has completed a *tack* within two overall lengths of the *mark* or *obstruction*; or when the *obstruction* is a continuing one as provided in rule 42.3(f).

(*b*) A yacht *clear ahead* shall be under no obligation to give room to a yacht *clear astern* before an *overlap* is established.

(c) When an outside yacht is *overlapped* at the time she comes within two of her overall lengths of a *mark* or an *obstruction*, she shall continue to be bound by rule 42.1(a), (Room at Marks and Obstructions when Overlapped), to give room as required even though the *overlap* may thereafter be broken.

(d) A yacht which claims an inside *overlap* has the onus of satisfying the race committee that the *overlap* was established in proper time.

(e) A yacht which claims to have broken an outside *overlap* has the onus of satisfying the race committee that she became *clear ahead* when she was more than two of her overall lengths from the *mark* of *obstruction*.

(f) A yacht *clear astern* may establish an *overlap* between the yacht *clear ahead* and a continuing *obstruction* such as a shoal or the shore or another vessel, only when at that time there is room for her to pass between them in safety.

42.4 AT A STARTING MARK SURROUNDED BY NAVIGABLE WATER
When approaching the starting line to *start*, a *leeward yacht* shall be under no obligation to give any *windward yacht* room to pass to leeward of a starting *mark* surrounded by navigable water; but, after the starting signal, a *leeward yacht* shall not deprive a *windward yacht* of room at such a *mark* by sailing either above the course to the first *mark* or above *close-hauled*.

43 Close-Hauled, Hailing for Room to Tack at Obstructions

43.1 HAILING
When two *close-hauled* yachts are on the same *tack* and safe pilotage requires the yacht *clear ahead* or the *leeward* yacht to make a substantial alteration of course to clear an *obstruction*, and she intends to *tack*, but cannot *tack* without colliding with the other yacht, she shall hail the other yacht for room to *tack* and clear the other yacht, but she shall not hail and *tack* simultaneously.

43.2 RESPONDING
The hailed yacht at the earliest possible moment after the hail shall:
either
(a) *tack*, in which case the hailing yacht shall begin to *tack* either:

(i) before the hailed yacht has completed her *tack*, or

(ii) if she cannot then *tack* without colliding with the hailed yacht, immediately she is able to *tack* and clear her;

or

(b) reply "You *tack*", or words to that effect, if in her opinion she can keep clear without *tacking* or after postponing her *tack*.
In this case:

(i) the hailing yacht shall immediately *tack* and

(ii) the hailed yacht shall keep clear.

(iii) The onus of satisfying the race committee that she kept clear shall lie on the hailed yacht which replied "You *tack*" to satisfy the race committee that she kept clear.

43.3 LIMITATIONS ON RIGHT TO ROOM WHEN THE OBSTRUCTION IS A MARK
(a) When the hailed yacht can fetch an *obstruction* which is also a *mark*, the hailing yacht shall not be entitled to room to *tack* and clear the hailed yacht and the hailed yacht shall immediately so inform the hailing yacht.

(b) If, thereafter, the hailing yacht again hails for room to *tack* and clear the hailed yacht she shall, after receiving room, retire immediately or exonerate herself by accepting an alternative penalty, when so prescribed in the sailing instructions.

(c) When, after having refused to respond to a hail under rule 43.3(a), the hailed yacht fails to fetch, she shall retire immediately, or exonerate herself by accepting an alternative penalty, when so prescribed in the sailing instructions.

44 Returning to Start

44.1 (a) After the starting signal is made, a premature starter returning to *start*, or a yacht working into position from the course side of the starting line or its extensions, shall keep clear of all yachts which are *starting* or have *started* correctly, until she is wholly on the pre-start side of the starting line or its extensions.

(b) Thereafter, she shall be accorded the rights under the rules of Part IV of a yacht which is *starting* correctly; but when she thereby acquires right of way over another yacht which is *starting* correctly, she shall allow that yacht ample room and opportunity to keep clear.

44.2 A premature starter while continuing to sail the course and until it is obvious that she is returning to *start*, shall be accorded the rights under the rules of Part IV of a yacht which has *started*.

45 Re-rounding after Touching a Mark

45.1 A yacht which has touched a *mark*, and is about to exonerate herself in accordance with rule 52.2, (Touching a Mark), shall keep clear of all other yachts which are about to round or pass it or have rounded or passed it correctly, until she has rounded it completely and has cleared it and is on a *proper course* to the next *mark*.

45.2 A yacht which has touched a *mark* while continuing to sail the course and until it is obvious that she is returning to round it completely in accordance with rule 52.2, (Touching a Mark), shall be accorded rights under the rules of Part IV.

46 Anchored, Aground or Capsized

46.1 A yacht under way shall keep clear of another yacht *racing* which is anchored, aground or capsized. Of two anchored yachts, the one which anchored later shall keep clear, except that a yacht which is dragging shall keep clear of one which is not.

46.2 A yacht anchored or aground shall indicate the fact to any yacht which may be in danger of fouling her. Unless the size of the yachts or the weather conditions make some other signal necessary, a hail is sufficient indication.

46.3 A yacht shall not be penalised for fouling a yacht in distress which she is attempting to assist or a yacht which goes aground or capsizes immediately ahead of her.

(Numbers 47, 48 and 49 are spare numbers)

PART V – Other Sailing Rules

Obligations of Helmsman and Crew in Handling a Yacht

A yacht is subject to the rules of Part V only while she is *racing*.

50   Ranking as a Starter

A yacht whose entry has been accepted by the race committee, which does not *start* but sails about in the vicinity of the starting line between her preparatory and starting signals shall rank as a starter.

51   Sailing the Course

51.1   (a) A yacht shall *start* and *finish* only as prescribed in the starting and finishing definitions.

(b) Unless otherwise prescribed in the sailing instructions, a yacht which either crosses prematurely, or is on the course side of the starting line, or its extensions, at the starting signal, shall return and *start* in accordance with the definition.

(c) Unless otherwise prescribed in the sailing instructions, when after a general recall, any part of a yacht's hull, crew or equipment is on the course side of the starting line or its extensions during the minute before her starting signal, she shall return to the pre-start side of the line across one of its extensions and *start*.

(d) Failure of a yacht to see or hear her recall notification shall not relieve her of her obligation to *start* correctly.

51.2   A yacht shall sail the course so as to round or pass each *mark* on the required side in correct sequence, and so that a string representing her wake from the time she *starts* until she *finishes* would, when drawn taut, lie on the required side of each *mark*.

51.3   A *mark* has a required side for a yacht as long as she is on a leg which it begins, bounds or ends. A starting line *mark* begins to have a required side for a yacht when she *starts*. A starting limit *mark* has a required side for a yacht from the time she is approaching the starting line to *start* until she has left the *mark* astern on the first leg. A finishing line *mark* and a finishing limit *mark* cease to have a required side for a yacht as soon as she *finishes*.

51.4   A yacht which rounds or passes a *mark* on the wrong side may exonerate herself by making her course conform to the requirements of rule 51.2.

51.5   It is not necessary for a yacht to cross the finishing line completely; after *finishing* she may clear it in either direction.

52   Touching a Mark

52.1   A yacht which:

either
(a) touches:

    (i) a starting *mark* before *starting*;

    (ii) a *mark* which begins, bounds or ends the leg of the course on which she is sailing; or

    (iii) a finishing *mark* after *finishing*;

or

(b) causes a *mark* or *mark* vessel to shift to avoid being touched, shall immediately retire, unless either:

    (i) she alleges that she was wrongfully compelled by another yacht to touch it or cause it to shift, in which case she shall act in accordance with rule 68.3, (Protests), unless the other yacht exonerates herself by accepting an alternative penalty when so prescribed in the sailing instructions, or

    (ii) she exonerates herself in accordance with rule 52.2.

52.2   (a) When a yacht touches a *mark* surrounded by navigable water, she may exonerate herself by completing one entire rounding of the *mark*, leaving it on the required side and thereafter re-rounding it or repassing it, without touching it, as required to sail the course in accordance with rule 51.2, (Sailing the Course), and the sailing instructions.

(b) When a yacht touches:

    (i) a starting *mark*, she shall carry out the rounding after she has *started*; or

    (ii) a finishing *mark*, she shall carry out the rounding, and she shall not rank as having *finished* until she has completed the rounding and again crosses the finishing line in accordance with the definition of *finishing*.

53   Fog Signals and Lights

Every yacht shall observe the International Regulations for Preventing Collisions at Sea or Government Rules for fog signals and, as a minimum, the carrying of lights at night.

54   Setting and Sheeting Sails

54.1   CHANGING SAILS
While changing headsails and spinnakers a replacing sail may be fully set and trimmed before the sail it replaces is taken in, but only one mainsail and, except when changing, only one spinnaker shall be carried set.

54.2   SHEETING SAILS TO SPARS
Unless otherwise prescribed by the national authority or by the class rules, any sail may be sheeted to or led above a boom regularly used for a working sail and permanently attached to the mast to which the head of the working sail is set, but no sails shall be sheeted over or through outriggers. An outrigger is any fitting so placed, except as permitted in the first sentence of rule 54.2, that it could exert outward pressure on a sheet at a point from which, with the yacht upright, a vertical line would fall outside the hull or deck planking at that point, or outside such other position as class rules prescribe. For the purpose of this rule: bulwarks, rails and rubbing strakes are not part of the hull or deck planking. A boom of a boomed headsail which requires no adjustment when *tacking* is not an outrigger.

54.3   SPINNAKER; SPINNAKER BOOM
A spinnaker shall not be set without a boom. The tack of a spinnaker when set and drawing shall be in close proximity to the outboard end of a spinnaker boom, any headsail may be attached to a spinnaker boom provided that a spinnaker is not set. A sail tacked down abaft the foremost mast is not a headsail. Only one spinnaker boom shall be used at a time and when in use shall be carried only on the side of the foremost mast opposite to the main boom and shall be fixed to the mast. Rule 54.3 shall not apply when shifting a spinnaker boom or sail attached thereto.

55   Owner Steering another Yacht

An owner shall not steer any yacht other than his own in a race wherein his own yacht competes, without the previous consent of the race committee.

56   Boarding

Unless otherwise prescribed by the national authority or in the sailing instructions, no person shall board a yacht except for the purposes of rule 58, (Rendering Assistance), or to attend an injured or ill member of the crew or temporarily as one of the crew of a vessel fouled.

57   Leaving, Man Overboard

Unless otherwise prescribed by the national authority or in the sailing instructions, no person on board a yacht when her preparatory signal was made shall leave, unless injured or ill, or for the purposes of rule 58, (Rendering Assistance), except that any member of the crew may fall overboard or leave her to swim, stand on the bottom as a means of anchoring, haul her out ashore to effect repairs, reef sails or bail out, or help her to get clear after grounding or fouling another vessel or object, provided that this person is back on board before the yacht continues in the race.

58   Rendering Assistance

Every yacht shall render all possible assistance to any vessel or person in peril, when in a position to do so.

59   Outside Assistance

Except as permitted by rules 56, (Boarding), 58, (Rendering Assistance), and 64, (Aground or Foul of an Obstruction), a yacht shall neither receive outside assistance nor use any gear other than that on board when her preparatory signal was made.

60   Means of Propulsion

60.1   A yacht shall be propelled only by the natural action of the wind on the sails, spars and hull, and water on the hull, and shall not promote or check way by abnormal means, except for the purposes of rule 58, (Rendering Assistance), or of recovering a person who has accidentally fallen overboard. An oar, paddle or other object may be used in emergency for steering. An anchor may be sent out in a boat only as permitted by rule 64, (Aground or Foul of an Obstruction).

60.2   "Pumping" and "ooching" shall be prohibited except under conditions established and defined in Appendix 2.

60.3   (Experimental rule for possible replacement of rule 60.2 and Appendix 2 before 1981)

(a) When so indicated in the sailing instructions rule 60.2 and Appendix 2 will be replaced by :
The following actions by a helmsman or crew shall constitute an infringement of rule 60.1 :

   (i) Repetitive frequent trimming and releasing of any sail(s).

   (ii) Repetitive forceful movement of the helm.

   (iii) Repetitive changing of the lateral or fore and aft trim of the yacht.

   (iv) Sudden movement of the crew weight fore and aft.

(b) When conditions of wind and water are such that the actions described in this rule are considered by the race committee to be a normal part of yacht racing, a signal to this effect (to be prescribed in the sailing instructions) shall be made by the race committee. When such a signal is made and for as long as it continues to be displayed, the actions described above shall not be prohibited. When the race committee considers that the conditions have changed sufficiently to prohibit these actions, a second signal (also to be prescribed in the sailing instructions) shall be displayed at the next turning *mark* about to be rounded by the class to which the signal applies. Such visual signal shall be accompanied by a repeated sound signal.

60.4 A yacht which hails before protesting under this rule helps to support her case.

61 Sounding

Any means of sounding may be used provided that rule 60, (Means of Propulsion), is not infringed.

62 Manual Power

A yacht shall use manual power only, except that when so prescribed by the national authority or in the sailing instructions, a power winch or windlass may be used in weighing anchor or in getting clear after running aground or fouling any object, and a power pump may be used in an auxiliary yacht.

63 Anchoring and Making Fast

63.1 BEFORE PREPARATORY SIGNAL
A yacht shall be afloat and off moorings, before her preparatory signal, but may be anchored, and shall not thereafter make fast or be made fast by means other than anchoring, nor be hauled out, except for the purpose of rule 64, (Aground or Foul of an Obstruction), or to effect repairs, reef sails or bail out.

63.2 WHEN RACING
A yacht may anchor. Means of anchoring may include the crew standing on the bottom and any weight lowered to the bottom. A yacht shall recover any anchor or weight used, and any chain or rope attached to it, before continuing in the race, unless after making every effort she finds recovery impossible. In this case she shall report the circumstances to the race committee, which may disqualify her if it considers the loss due either to inadequate gear or to insufficient effort to recover it.

64 Aground or Foul of an Obstruction

A yacht, after grounding or fouling another vessel or other object, is subject to rule 62, (Manual Power), and may, in getting clear, use her own anchors, boats, ropes, spars and other gear; may send out an anchor in a boat; may be refloated by her crew going overboard either to stand on the bottom or to go ashore to push off; but may receive outside assistance only from the crew of the vessel fouled. A yacht shall recover all her own gear used in getting clear before continuing in the race.

65 Skin Friction

A yacht shall not eject or release from a container any substance (such as polymer) the purpose of which is, or could be, to reduce the frictional resistance of the hull by altering the character of the flow of water inside the boundary layer.

66 Increasing Stability

Unless otherwise prescribed by her class rules or in the sailing instructions, a yacht shall not use any device, such as a trapeze or plank, to project outboard the weight of any of the crew, nor, when lifelines are required by the conditions for the race, shall any member of the crew station any part of his torso outside them, other than temporarily.

(Number 67 is a spare number)

PART VI – **Protests, Disqualifications and Appeals**

68   Protests

68.1   A yacht can protest against any other yacht, except that a protest for an alleged infringement of the rules of Part IV can be made only by a yacht directly involved in, or witnessing an incident.

68.2   A protest occurring between yachts competing in separate races sponsored by different clubs shall be heard by a combined committee of the clubs concerned.

68.3   (a) A protest for an infringement of the rules or sailing instructions occurring during a race shall be signified by the protesting yacht conspicuously displaying a flag (International Code flag "B" is always acceptable, irrespective of any other provisions in the sailing instructions) at the first reasonable opportunity and keeping it displayed until she has *finished* or retired, or if the first reasonable opportunity occurs after *finishing*, until acknowledged by the race committee. In the case of a yacht sailed single-handed, it will be sufficient if the flag be displayed at the first reasonable opportunity and brought to the notice of the race committee when the protesting yacht *finishes*.

(b) A yacht which has no knowledge of the facts justifying a protest, including the failure of another yacht to lodge a required protest, until after she has *finished* or retired may nevertheless protest without having displayed a protest flag.

(c) A protesting yacht shall try to inform the yacht protested against that a protest will be lodged.

(d) Such a protest shall be in writing and be signed by the owner or his representative, and include the following particulars:

(i) The date, time and whereabouts of the incident.

(ii) The particular rule or rules or sailing instructions alleged to have been infringed.

(iii) A statement of the facts.

(iv) Unless irrelevant, a diagram of the incident.

(e) Unless otherwise prescribed in the sailing instructions a protesting yacht shall deliver or, if that is not possible, mail her protest to the race committee :

(i) within two hours of the time she *finishes* the race or within such time as may have been prescribed in the sailing instructions under rule 3.2(b)(xv), (The Sailing Instructions), unless the race committee has reason to extend these time limits, or

(ii) when she does not *finish* the race, within such a time as the race committee may consider reasonable in the circumstances of the case. A protest shall be accompanied by such fee, if any, as may have been prescribed in the sailing instructions under rule 3.2(b)(xv), (The Sailing Instructions).

(f) The race committee shall allow the protestor to remedy at a later time :

(i) any defects in the details required by rule 68.3(d) provided that the protest includes a summary of the facts, and

(ii) a failure to deposit such fee as may be required under rule 68.3(e) and prescribed in the sailing instructions.

68.4 (a) A protest that a measurement, scantling or flotation rule has been infringed while *racing*, or that a classification or rating certificate is for any reason invalid, shall be lodged with the race committee not later than 18.00 hours on the day following the race. The race committee shall send a copy of the protest to the yacht protested against and, when there appears to be reasonable grounds for the protest, it shall refer the question to an authority qualified to decide such questions.

(b) Deviations in excess of tolerances stated in the class rules caused by normal wear or damage and which do not affect the performance of the yacht shall not invalidate the measurement or rating certificate of the yacht for a particular race, but shall be rectified before she *races* again, unless in the opinion of the race committee there has been no practical opportunity to rectify the wear or damage.

(c) The race committee, in making its decision, shall be governed by the determination of such authority. Copies of such decision shall be sent to all yachts involved.

68.5 (a) A yacht which alleges that her finishing position has been materially prejudiced by an action or omission of the race committee, may seek redress from the race committee in accordance with the requirements for a protest provided in rules 68.3(d), (e) and (f). In these circumstances a protest flag need not be displayed.

(b) When the race committee decides that such action or omission was prejudicial, and that the result of the race was altered thereby, it shall make such arrangement as it deems equitable, which may be to let the results of the race stand ; or to *abandon* or *cancel* the race, provided that the race committee shall not act under this rule before satisfying itself by taking appropriate evidence that its action is as equitable as possible as far as all competitors are concerned, for that particular race and the series, if any, as a whole.

68.6 A protest made in writing shall not be withdrawn, but shall be decided by the race committee, unless prior to the hearing full responsibility is acknowledged by one or more yachts.

69 Refusal of a Protest

69.1 When the race committee decides that a protest does not conform to the requirements of rule 68, (Protests), it shall inform the protesting yacht that her protest will not be heard and of the reasons for such decision.

69.2 Such a decision shall not be reached without giving the protesting yacht an opportunity of bringing evidence that the requirements of rule 68, (Protests), were complied with.

70 Hearings

70.1 When the race committee decides that a protest conforms to all the requirements of rule 68, (Protests), it shall call a hearing as soon as possible. The protest, or a copy of it, shall be made available to all yachts involved, and each shall be notified, in writing if practicable, of the time and place set for the hearing. A reasonable time shall be allowed for the preparation of defence. At the hearing, the race committee shall take the evidence presented by the parties to the protest and such other evidence as it may consider necessary. The parties to the protest, or a representative of each, shall have the right to be present, but all others, except one witness at a time while testifying, may be excluded. A yacht other than one named in the protest, which is involved in that protest, shall have all the rights of yachts originally named in it.

70.2 A yacht shall not be penalised without a hearing, except as provided in rules 73.1(a), (Race Committee's Action against an Infringing Yacht).

70.3 Failure on the part of any of the interested parties or a representative to make an effort to attend the hearing of the protest may justify the race committee in deciding the protest as it thinks fit without a full hearing.

70.4 For the purpose of rule 70, the word "protest" shall include, when appropriate, an investigation of redress under rule 12, (Yacht Materially Prejudiced) ; a request for redress under rule 68.5, (Protests) ; or a notification of an infringement hearing under rule 73, (Race Committee's Action against an Infringing Yacht).

70.5 When *abandonment* or *cancellation* of a completed race is under con-
sideration by the race committee, the race committee shall not act before
satisfying itself by taking appropriate evidence that its action is as equitable
as possible as far as all competitors are concerned, for that particular race
and the series, if any, as a whole.

71 Decisions

The race committee shall make its decisions promptly after the hearing. Each
decision shall be communicated to the parties involved, and shall state fully
the facts and grounds on which it is based and shall specify the rules, if any,
infringed. When requested by any of the parties, such decision shall be given
in writing and shall include the race committee's diagram. The findings of the
race committee as to the facts involved shall be final.

72 Disqualification after Protest and Liability for Damages

72.1 When the race committee, after hearing a protest or acting under rule 73,
(Race Committee's Action against an Infringing Yacht), or any appeal
authority, is satisfied :

(a) that a yacht has infringed any of these rules or the sailing instructions, or

(b) that in consequence of her neglect of any of these rules or the sailing
instructions she has compelled other yachts to infringe any of these rules or
the sailing instructions, she shall be disqualified unless the sailing instructions applicable to that race provide some other penalty. Such disqualification or other penalty shall be imposed, irrespective of whether the rule or
sailing instruction which led to the disqualification or penalty was mentioned
in the protest, or the yacht which was at fault was mentioned or protested
against, e.g., the protesting yacht or a third yacht might be disqualified and
the protested yacht absolved.

72.2 For the purpose of awarding points in a series, a retirement after an infringement of any of these rules or the sailing instructions shall not rank as a
disqualification. This penalty can be imposed only in accordance with rules
72, (Disqualification after Protest), and 73, (Race Committee's Action
against an Infringing Yacht).

72.3 When a yacht either is disqualified or has retired, the next in order shall be
awarded her place.

72.4 Alternative Penalties. When so prescribed in the sailing instructions, the
procedure and penalty for infringing a rule of Part IV shall be as provided in
Appendix 3, Alternative Penalties for Infringement of a Rule of Part IV.

72.5 The question of damages arising from an infringement of any of these rules
or the sailing instructions shall be governed by the prescriptions, if any, of
the national authority.

73 Race Committee's Action Against an Infringing Yacht

73.1 WITHOUT A HEARING

(a) A yacht which fails either to *start* or to *finish* may be disqualified without a protest or hearing, after the conclusion of the race, except that she shall be entitled to a hearing, if she satisfies the race committee that an error may have been made.

(b) A yacht so penalized shall be informed of the action taken, either by letter or by notification in the racing results.

73.2 WITH A HEARING

When the race committee:

(a) sees an apparent infringement by a yacht of any of these rules or the sailing instructions (except as provided in rule 73.1), or

(b) learns directly from a written or oral statement by a yacht that she may have infringed a rule or sailing instruction, or

(c) has reasonable grounds for believing that an infringement resulted in serious damage, or

(d) receives a report not later than the same day from a witness who was neither competing in the race, nor otherwise an interested party, alleging an infringement, or

(e) has reasonable grounds for supposing from the evidence at the hearing of a valid protest, or a hearing called in accordance with rule 73.2, that any yacht involved in the incident may have committed an infringement, the race committee may notify such yacht thereof orally, or if that is not possible, in writing, delivered or mailed not later than 18.00 hours on the day after:

(i) the finish of the race, or

(ii) the receipt of the report, or

(iii) the hearing of the protest.

Such notice shall contain a statement of the pertinent facts and of the particular rule or rules or sailing instructions believed to have been infringed, and the race committee shall act thereon in the same manner as if it had been a protest made by a competitor.

74 Penalties for Gross Infringement of Rules or Misconduct

74.1 When a gross infringement of any of these rules, the sailing instructions or class rules is proved against the owner, the owner's representative, the helmsman or a crew of a yacht, such persons may be disqualified by the national authority, for any period it may think fit, from either steering or sailing in a yacht in any race held under its jurisdiction.
Notice of any penalty adjudged under this rule may be communicated by the national authority to the I.Y.R.U. which shall inform all national authorities.

74.2 After a gross breach of good manners or sportsmanship the race committee may exclude a competitor either from further participation in a series or from the whole series or take other disciplinary action.

75 Persons Interested not to take part in Decision

75.1 No member of either a race committee or of any appeals authority shall take part in the discussion or decision upon any disputed question in which he is an interested party, but this does not preclude him from giving evidence in such a case.

75.2 The term "interested party" includes anyone who stands to gain or lose as a result of the decision.

76 Expenses Incurred by Protest

Unless otherwise prescribed by the race committee, the fees and expenses entailed by a protest on measurement or classification shall be paid by the unsuccessful party.

77 Appeals

77.1 Unless otherwise prescribed by the national authority which has recognised the organising authority concerned, an appeal against the decision of a race committee shall be governed by rules 77, (Appeals), and 78, (Particulars to be Supplied in Appeals).

77.2 Unless otherwise prescribed by the national authority or in the sailing instructions (subject to rule 2(j), (Notice of Race), or 3.2(b)(xvii), (Waiver of Appeal)), a protest which has been decided by the race committee shall be referred to the national authority solely on a question of interpretation of these rules, within such period after the receipt of the race committee's decision as the national authority may decide:

(a) when the race committee, at its own instance, thinks proper to do so, or

(b) when any of the parties involved in the protest makes application for such reference.

This reference shall be accompanied by such deposit as the national authority may prescribe, payable by the appellant, to be forfeited to the funds of the national authority in the event of the appeal being dismissed.

77.3 The national authority shall have power to uphold or reverse the decision of the race committee, and if it is of opinion, from the facts found by the race committee, that a yacht involved in a protest has infringed an applicable rule, it shall disqualify her, irrespective of whether the rule or sailing instruction which led to such disqualification was mentioned in the protest.

77.4 For the purpose of rule 77, the word "protest" shall include, when appropriate, an investigation of redress under rule 12, (Yacht Materially Prejudiced); a request for redress under rule 68.5, (Protests); or a notification of an infringement hearing under rule 73, (Race Committee's Action against an Infringing Yacht).

77.5 The decision of the national authority, which shall be final, shall be communicated in writing to all interested parties.

77.6 Decisions of an international jury shall be final, provided that the Terms of Reference of an International Jury and the Conditions for the Decision of an International Jury or Protest Committee to be Final, as set forth in Appendices 8 and 9, are observed :

(a) In the Olympic Regatta and similar regattas open to yachts from different nations and in such other international regattas as may be under the jurisdiction of the I.Y.R.U. or a national authority, or

(b) In other international regattas under the jurisdiction of an international class association, with the approval of the national authority when required.

77.7 An appeal once lodged with the national authority shall not be withdrawn.

78 Particulars to be Supplied in Appeals

78.1 The reference to the national authority shall be in writing and shall contain the following particulars, in order, so far as they are applicable :

(a) A copy of the notice of the race and the sailing instructions supplied to the yachts.

(b) A copy of the protest, or protests or request for redress under rule 12, (Yacht Materially Prejudiced) or rule 68.5(a), (Protests), if any, prepared in accordance with rule 68.3(d), and all other written statements which may have been put in by the parties.

(c) The observations of the race committee thereon, a full statement of the facts found, its decision and the grounds thereof.

(d) An official diagram prepared by the race committee in accordance with the facts found by it, showing :

(i) The course to the next *mark*, or, if close by, the *mark* itself with the required side ;

(ii) the direction and force of the wind ;

(iii) the set and strength of the tidal stream or current, if any ;

(iv) the depth of water, if relevant ; and

(v) the positions and courses of all the yachts involved ;

(vi) it is preferable to show yachts sailing from the bottom of the diagram towards the top.

(e) The grounds of the appeal, to be supplied by either :

(i) the race committee under rule 77.2(a) ; or

(ii) the appellant under rule 77.2(b).

(f) Observations, if any, upon the appeal by the race committee or any of the parties.

78.2 The race committee shall notify all parties that an appeal will be lodged and shall invite them to make any observations upon it. Any such observations shall be forwarded with the appeal.

APPENDIX 2 – "Pumping" Sails, "Ooching" and "Rocking"

"Pumping" consists of frequent rapid trimming of sails with no particular reference to a change in true or apparent wind direction. To promote planing or surfing, rapid trimming of sails need not be considered "pumping".

The purpose of this interpretation of rule 60, (Means of Propulsion), is to prevent "fanning" one's boat around the course by flapping the sail similar to a bird's wing in flight. "Pumping" or frequent, quickly-repeated trimming and releasing of the mainsail to increase propulsion is not allowed and is not "the natural action of the wind on the sails".

Similarly, frequent, quickly-repeated gybing or roll-tacking in calm and near calm conditions fall into the same category as "pumping".

Where surfing or planing conditions exist, however, rule 60 allows taking advantage of "the natural action of water on the hull" through the rapid trimming of sails and adjustment of helm to promote (initiate) surfing or planing.

The test is whether or not the conditions are such that by rapid trimming of sails a boat could be started surfing or planing. A skipper challenged for "pumping" will have to prove, through the performance either of his own boat or of other boats, that surfing or planing conditions existed, and that the frequency of his rapid trimming was geared to the irregular or cyclical wave forms rather than to a regular rhythmic pattern.

Note that the interpretation refers to "promoting" and not to "maintaining" surfing or planing. Once a boat has started surfing or planing on a particular set of wave forms, from then on she must let the natural action of wind and water propel her without further rapid trimming and releasing of the sails.

Rapid trimming when approaching marks or the finishing line or other critical points should be consistent with that which was practised throughout the leg.

"Ooching", which consists of lunging forward and stopping abruptly, falls into the same category as "pumping".

"Rocking" consists of persistently rolling a yacht from side to side.

APPENDIX 3 – Alternative penalties for an infringement of a rule of Part IV

Experience indicates that the 720° turns penalty is most satisfactory for small boats in relatively short races, but that it can be dangerous for large yachts and in restricted waters and not sufficiently severe in long races. The 20% penalty is relatively mild and is designed to encourage acknowledgement of infringements and willingness to protest when not acknowledged. Both systems keep yachts racing.

Either of the following alternatives to disqualification may be used by including in the sailing instructions a provision such as the following (or if preferred the selected penalty may be quoted in full) :

"The 720° turns penalty (or the percentage penalty) as provided in rule 72.4, Disqualification after Protest and Liability for Damages, Alternative Penalties, and Appendix 5, Alternative Penalties for Infringement of a Rule of Part IV, of the yacht racing rules shall apply, instead of disqualification, for infringement of a rule of Part IV."

1 720° Turns

A yacht which acknowledges infringing a rule of Part IV, may exonerate herself by making two full 360° turns (720°), subject to the following provisions :

1.1   When the yacht infringed against intends to protest, she shall notify the infringing yacht at the first reasonable opportunity by hail and by displaying a protest flag. (The first reasonable opportunity for a hail is usually immediately.)

1.2   At the first reasonable opportunity after such notification, or without such notification when a yacht realises she has infringed a rule of Part IV, the yacht acknowledging fault shall make her turns. While doing so, she shall keep clear of all other yachts until she has completed her turns and is on a *proper course* for the next *mark*.

1.3   The turns may be made in either direction but both in the same direction, with the second full circle following immediately on the first.

1.4   When the infringement occurs before the starting signal is made, the infringing yacht shall make her turns after the starting signal is made.

1.5   When an infringement occurs at the finishing line, the infringing yacht shall make her turns on the last leg of the course before being officially finished.

1.6   If neither yacht acknowledges fault, a protest may be lodged in accordance with rule 68, (Protests), and the sailing instructions.

1.7   Failure to observe the above requirements will render a yacht which has infringed a rule of Part IV liable to disqualification or other penalty, but when an infringing yacht's turns do not conform with the above requirements, the yacht infringed against is relieved of further obligations under rule 33.2, (Contact between Yachts Racing).

1.8   An infringing yacht involved in a collision which results in serious damage to either yacht shall be liable to disqualification.

1.9   The race committee may disqualify a yacht for an infringement of the rules which results in an advantage to the infringing yacht after completing the 720° turns, whether or not serious damage results. The race committee's action shall be governed by rule 73, (Race Committee's Action against an Infringing Yacht).

2   Percentage

2.1   A yacht which acknowledges infringing a rule of Part IV shall be penalised by receiving the score for the place worse than her actual finishing position by 20% to the nearest whole number of the number of starters in that race, except that the penalty shall be at least three places and except further that in no case shall she receive a score for a position worse than one more than the number of starters. (Examples : An infringing yacht which finishes eighth in a start of nineteen yachts will receive the score for twelfth place (19 × 0.2 + 3.8 or 4) ; an infringing yacht which finishes thirteenth in a start of fourteen yachts will receive the score for fifteenth place.)

(a) A yacht infringing a rule in more than one incident shall receive a 20% penalty for each incident.

(b) The imposition of a 20% penalty on a yacht shall not affect the score of other yachts. (Thus two yachts may receive the same score.)

2.2   A yacht which acknowledges infringing a rule of Part IV shall at the first reasonable opportunity display International Code flag "I", or such other signal as the sailing instructions may specify, keep it flying until she has *finished* and report the infringement to the race committee.

2.3   When the yacht infringed against intends to protest, she shall notify the infringing yacht at the first reasonable opportunity by hail and by displaying a protest flag. (The first reasonable opportunity for a hail is usually immediately.)

2.4   A yacht which fails to acknowledge an infringement as provided in paragraph 2.2 and which, after a protest and hearing, is found to have infringed a rule of Part IV, shall be penalised 50% or at least five places instead of 20%.

2.5   A yacht which has displayed International Code flag "I" during a race and has not reported the infringement to the race committee shall be liable to the

50% penalty of paragraph 2.4 without a hearing except on the two points of having displayed the flag and having reported the infringement to the race committee.

2.6   An infringing yacht involved in a collision which results in serious damage to either yacht shall be liable to disqualification.
The race committee may disqualify a yacht for a serious infringement of the rules, whether or not serious damage resulted.

APPENDIX 6 – Protest Committee Procedure

Rules Concerning Protests – 68, 69, 70, 71, 72, 73 and 75

In a protest hearing, the race committee should give equal weight to the testimony of all principals; should recognise that honest testimony can vary and even be in conflict as a result of different observations or recollections; should resolve such differences as best it can; should recognise that no yacht is guilty until her infringement has been established to the satisfaction of the race committee; should keep an open mind until all the evidence has been submitted as to whether the protestor or the protestee or a third yacht, if one is involved in the incident, has infringed a rule.

Preliminaries

1   Note on the protest the time at which it is received.

2   Determine whether the protest contains the information called for by rule 68.3(d) in sufficient detail to identify the incident and to tell the recipient what the protest is about. If not, ask the protestor to supply the information (rule 68.3(f)).

3   Unless the protest already provides the information
Inquire whether the protestor flew a protest flag in accordance with rule 68.3(a) unless rule 68.3(b) applies or the protestor is seeking redress under rule 68.5(a) and note his answer on the protest.

4   Unless the protest already provides the information
Inquire whether the protestor tried to inform the yacht(s) protested against (the protestee(s)) that a protest would be lodged (rule 68.3(c)) and note his answer on the protest.
See that the protest fee (if any) required by the sailing instructions is included and note its receipt on the protest.

5   When the protest conforms to the requirements of rule 68 (see 1, 2 and 3 above), arrange to hold a hearing as soon as possible. Notify the representative of each yacht involved of the time and place of the hearing (rule 70.1).

7   When possible, it is very desirable that photocopies of the protest be made available to all the parties.

The Hearing

1   The representative of each yacht involved in the incident (with a language interpreter, if needed) is entitled to be present throughout the hearing. All

others, except one witness at a time while testifying, may be excluded (rule 70.1).

2   Read to the meeting the protest and any other written statement there may be about the incident (such as an account of it from the protestee).

3   Invite first the protestor and then the protestee(s) to give their accounts of the incident. Each may question the other(s). Questions by the protest committee, except for clarifying details, are preferably deferred until all accounts have been presented. Models are useful. Positions before and after the incident itself are often helpful.

4   Invite first the protestor and then the protestee to call witnesses. They may be questioned by the protestor and protestee(s) as well as by the committee.

5   Invite first the protestor and then the protestee to make a final statement of his case, including any application or interpretation of the rules to the incident as he sees it.

Decision

1   The protest committee, after dismissing those involved in the incident, should decide what the relevant facts are.

2   The committee should then apply the rules and reach a decision as to who, if anyone, infringed a rule and what rule was infringed (rule 71).

3   Having reached a decision in writing, recall the protestor and protestee and read to them the facts from the decision and the grounds for it (rule 71).

4   Any party involved is entitled to a copy of the decision (rule 71), signed by the chairman of the protest committee. A copy should also be filed with the committee records.

    N.B. The protest committee referred to above may be the race committee or the jury appointed for the event in which the incident occurred or a protest committee established by the race committee for the express purpose of hearing protests.